Get Back on the Horse?

Susan R. Scott

Susan R. Scott

Get Back on the Horse? is a must read for anyone who desires to escape the feeling of being alone, stuck in a rut somewhere out in the desert of life, and wants to somehow re-fire the intimate and courageous adventure of following Christ.

Sue's candid conversations with the Lord, and playful (yet practical) stories, eloquently illustrate not only the true nature of God, but how His grace is powerful enough to lift up even the weariest, brushing off every burden, and making the ride joyful again — a ride into His amazing purpose for their lives!

I've read this book twice now, and each time the fire in my heart has ignited with greater passion to know Jesus and make Him known.

Rev. Kevin MacDonald
River of Life Christian Fellowship

For Claudia ~

May your legacy of compassion

and encouragement live on…

CONTENTS

INTRO: In a Nutshell (A Very Large Nutshell)

Have you ever set up a story you're about to tell in such a detailed way that you rabbit trail your point right off the page and then suddenly don't have a clue where you were headed? Okay, so maybe it's just me, but for the moment I'll try to stay on track and leave the rabbit trails for later.

It seems my life is a walking metaphor. I listen and process with my heart and then breathe in and exhale with "well, it's kinda like…." Every lesson I learn is "kinda like" something else to me. So, for anyone else who understands by metaphors, take heart — Jesus taught in parables, which is just a fancy word for "kinda likes." "The Kingdom of Heaven is like…" So see? We're not the only ones.

Life is kinda like a book. It's just a series of smaller stories, pages of ideas, words, experiences and perspectives, pasted and bound together along a common edge. What's so hard about writing a book? It's kinda like life — it just happens. You have to gather it all together, find the glue, and make it readable. Ta-da!

And so the rabbit trail begins…

Chapter 1: From Fairy Tales to Bunny Trails

I've heard it said that most writers are avid readers. Truth is, I never liked to read. [This is really still part of the "very large nutshell" introduction, but I tend to skip over introductions so I made this Chapter 1.] I don't like to read, but I love to be read to. Even as a child, I loved how words could paint a picture and make me feel things. I loved listening to stories and seeing them acted out. It inspired me to act out the stories myself, first with my childhood friends, then in school plays and musicals with my teenage friends. This led me to children's theatre and community theatre with my young adult friends, and ultimately brought me to writing and directing for friends of all ages. For 20 years I wrote plays and sketches as sermon illustrations, kid's curriculum, and church theatre productions (some of which are included in this book).

Songs often carried or completed the storylines for me. Music carries truth straight to my heart. I began to write more and more of my own lyrics to convey the desired message and found I had to listen really closely to hear just the right words that God was whispering. He and I both know I'm not a gifted writer. I'm just a good listener.

For me, writing this book is all about being a good listener. Anything that touches your heart in this book is because you've been listening, too. You've heard God say it to you already and when you see it in print, it confirms and waters something in you that He's already planted. It may challenge an idea that's been germinating or even one you've been dearly holding onto for a long time. Sometimes words/poetry can repaint the picture or carry a truth to your heart, almost like music would. Once there, God can use it to bring clarity and give you a new perspective.

God once said to me, "Will you listen? Stop thinking and just listen. The trees will tell you; I move as I see fit and dance with their leaves. How much more will My Spirit dance with yours — Creator with creator? I gave you everything, everything I own. See, I'm handing it to you. You just don't have room enough for it. Downsize a bit. Pass on the truth you treasure to someone else. Trade with Me. Trust Me with your most prized possession, and I'll give you Mine."

It's hard to give away something you love, especially something you've made or invested in or put your heart and soul into. Most artists will tell you that when you release creativity into the atmosphere, it's like a piece of you is suddenly on display. To release it into the scrutiny of the public eye can be intimidating if not downright frightening for some of us. Especially for those of us who have, let's say "discriminating" taste and tend to easily "discern" flaws and imperfections. We can become overly-sensitive, dare I say paranoid, about our audience's potential tomato-throwing disapproval. So why would someone like that EVER write a book?

For the last six years the only writing I've done has been inconsistent journaling here and there and LOTS of texting. And for a couple of years now, whenever my husband, Steve, would see me writing in a notebook he'd tease me with, "How's our book coming?" A few years back, a young man had spoken a prophetic word to him that he saw Steve writing a book. We both laughed at the thought because as skillful as Steve is at many things, writing is not his forte. But he has always skillfully deciphered and typed out hundreds and hundreds of pages over the years of my handwritten stories and scripts (typing is not my forte). So we decided it must have been "our" book that the young man saw Steve typing.

Writing in a journal is one thing (you're the only one who reads it) or even writing scripts and stories for your church family to enjoy... but writing a book? How in the world did I get here?

As I looked back over my inconsistent and scattered journal entries, they so clearly spelled out to me what God wanted me to do. It's almost embarrassing that it took me so long to see it. It's like my journal of a journey that I didn't even know I was on:

January 2016

So here I am standing (mostly sitting) on the edge of an unknown project, feeling all kinds of feelings, overwhelmed and a little excited. I'm fighting voices of inadequacy, fear, and shame. I'm ready to do what I can with what I have, but I have no idea what the project even is. In all of it, I think I'm learning to be more honest with myself — to not pretend I have any answers, or even a clue that I know what I'm doing. All I know is that You'll supply all my needs as I give away what I have, with a heart that's trying to support and help others. God, I just want to write down for the record that all those people I know and love, struggling with depression and the after effects of trauma, are weighing heavy on my heart and I want to see them FREE! Please show me my part. I'm so angry with the darkness. Empower me to be effective in this battle that rages against Your precious kids. Catch my tears and drown the enemy with them.

Then I heard God say, "Isaiah 49:9." I looked it up. Starting at verse 8 it reads: In the time of My favor I will answer you and in the day of salvation I will help you... to say to the captives, "Come out" and to those in darkness, "Be free!"

May 9, 2016

I'm about to walk through the door, a door opened to me by God, Himself. I'm writing this down because He told me to, in ink, not to be corrected or erased or criticized.

I love writing by hand. I've texted so much lately I forgot how this feels. It's almost like drawing. That's what God's doing. He's bringing me someplace I've never been but to do something I've been doing my whole life, something He's designed me to do — like writing in pen. It's something that can't be erased or doesn't have to be perfect, but will still be effective.

October 31, 2016

God said to me, "I gave you the ability to see things metaphorically. It's like seeing into the spiritual realm — to see the spirit, the essence, the idea behind, the similarity, the purpose, the "kinda like." Don't apologize or be embarrassed by it. It's a piece of Me and I've placed it in you, not because you're better or special, but just because I like to share and you're designed to hold this one and to use it. Now use it. Enjoy it. Don't be burdened by it. Love it!"

March 10, 2017

I'm questioning my motivation, or even my desire, to write a book. Is it even possible to write an inspired book if you have no desire to? Can you undertake such a huge project because other people keep telling you, "You should"? Only obedience to a Love you believe in can trump "lack of desire." Obey and He'll give you the desire. But is GOD telling me to write a book?

Five days later, March 15, 2017, God told me to read "The Elijah List" for that day (www.elijahlist.com). I laughed and cried at His kindness and grace as I read Angie Stolba's article, "Full Bloom: A Season of Promises Being Fulfilled." This is an excerpt:

In this season, God is calling forth the scribes of His Heart — those who have been carrying His treasure of wisdom and revelation from on High. "You will write, write and write some

4

more. The words I give you will be spirit and life. They will penetrate hearts and set captives free!" says the Lord of Hosts. I see pens on fire and manuscripts coming forth...dust off the promises and prophetic words that have been spoken over your life. [www.angiestolba.com]

Write the book!

And then as if to make sure I got the message, the following Sunday the prophet/evangelist at the church we were attending had a word for anyone who liked riding horses or who used to ride. Now you've got to understand — I LOVE horses! I rode as a kid and have always had awe and respect for their magnificence and beauty. My first drawings and paint-by-numbers were of horses. My childhood bedroom was wallpapered with horses. There is a connection there, a love for horses that is so over the top in comparison with just regular likes and dislikes.

I could never understand why my parents wouldn't let us at least have a pony. We had a perfectly good garage that it could live in. I'd take care of it, I promised. All the other kids (in our suburban neighborhood) could chip in, too. Their answer was still "No." But those two loving, sacrificial souls gave up more than I'll ever know so that my sister and I could, if nothing else, take riding lessons. I had no clue then how much we lived paycheck to paycheck.

Those loving, giving parents ended up moving in with my husband and me in 2007 so we could assist them and care for my mom who had developed Alzheimer's three years before. For seven years we fought to keep them at home with us. We prayed and believed for complete healing, daily. We fought nightly battles with demons of fear and confusion. God's grace carried us. We saw Him heal and deliver them both from so very much, as He was equipping and training us for spiritual battle, on the job, 24/7.

But when my mom's condition became dangerous to us all, including herself, and my dad at age 83, developed congestive heart failure requiring oxygen tubing that could potentially trip my mom, we had to get them into a professional care facility. I thought leaving them there would kill me. God assured me with all kinds of miraculous confirmations it was His provision and plan and that the dementia unit would be their final mission field. This is what I wrote in a notebook on August 12, 2014, four months after we placed them there (and what turned out to be one month before my father passed):

> Face the giants with shoulders back and head covered with salvation. This day has been made by God. Rejoice in it. Flow in it. Float in it. Don't look back. Don't diminish what God is expanding in you. Climb high. Reach up. Grab hold.
>
> The ledge is there, you just can't see it. Hold on too tightly to where you are and it will crumble beneath you. Rise up. Breathe deep and rise up. Don't look down. Don't look back, but know the mountain is beneath you, and the eagle is soaring above you. "Come, My Beloved, come soar on wings as eagles." One last thrust of effort. One more stretch and this mountain will be conquered.
>
> Remember Who's got you. Remember Whose you are. Remember your dream to dance and to fly. That's why you love the horse to gallop, because all his feet leave the ground at once and you're flying. For seconds at a time you're relying on the power beneath you to lift you off the ground to carry you into your destiny — to fly. You're trusting in both the strength and the submission of the power beneath you. You're not able to soar without first trusting that the power could crush you, but instead carries you. Don't let go. Don't try to understand. Just fly with your eyes fixed ahead and your head lifted up. Flow... Flow... Flow...

So on Sunday night, March 19, 2017 when the prophetic evangelist called those of us who liked to ride horses to the front to give us a word from God, I knew God was up to something. Just the day before I had found my old notebook and read the August 2014 entry. This is what God spoke to me through Kevin MacDonald that night:

"Get back on the horse! You need to get back on the horse! Come on!" He says, "You need to get back on the horse! You're walking alongside the horse and you're weary and tired and I've provided you a horse to take you where you need to go. Stop being stubborn…" There is a supernatural provision for you because you are aware of what it feels like to ride on a horse's back. The Spirit will carry you to your destination… You've been chosen tonight because you understand that intimate connection…

 between rider and horse. If you've ever looked into a horse's eyes you know there's more in there than just a creature. There's a living breathing emotional connection that happens. The Holy Spirit is bringing you into… a deeper more intimate connection in your walk with God, or shall I say your "ride" with God, because you'll be riding on the Holy Spirit… You're lame because you've been walking too far… So the Lord is carrying you for a season. You're not unworthy because you're injured. He's carrying you because you ARE worthy… I encourage you to write some of this down to remember it… all you have to do is get up on the horse.

Hence the title — this book is all about getting back on, for anyone who's fallen off and gotten the wind knocked out of them by life or lies or loss.

My hope is that these stories, sketches and lyrics will be "spirit and life," that "they will penetrate hearts and set captives free" and that you will be inspired to get back on the horse again… and fly.

Chapter 1: From Fairy Tales to Bunny Trails

Chapter 2: Growing Pains /RECONSTRUCTION

SCENE: Two young women, Darlene and Kim, standing on the porch of a house, early fall. There are empty clay pots along the porch railing. A baby is heard crying offstage. Darlene is patiently watching Kim, who's trying to get out the door.

[LIGHTS UP]

KIM (To baby offstage): I'll be right back Adam. I promise. Mommy's gonna go get you birthday surprises. [Leaning offstage] Okay. One more hug. [Then back onstage] I'll be right back. Be good for Melissa, don't cry now. (To babysitter) His bottle's in the refrigerator. We won't be long. Bye, Adam. Mommy loves you. I'll be back, I promise. [Shuts the door and listens]

DARLENE: Come on, he'll be fine. It's only for, not even an hour.

KIM: I know, but that'll seem like days to him… and Melissa too if he doesn't settle down.

DARLENE: He'll be fine. [Encourages Kim toward stairs] The sooner we leave the sooner we can come back.

KIM: [Back to door] He just doesn't understand. He's crying like he's never gonna see me again.

DARLENE: Well is he gonna see you again?

KIM: Of course.

DARLENE: And you're not gonna come home empty-handed. You're gonna bring all kinds of wonderful birthday surprises for him, right?

KIM (Weakly): Yeah.

DARLENE: And he'll be so happy to see you, he'll forget you had ever left.

KIM: Okay.

DARLENE: But you can't come back and make him happy if you don't leave first.

KIM: Okay, you're right. Let's go. He'll be fine.

DARLENE: He will be ya know.

KIM [Stops at plant pots, looks at them and scoldingly says]: Hey! What's taking so long? Any day now, huh? Grow will ya!

DARLENE: Why are you yelling at the pots of dirt?

KIM: There's bulbs in there (To plant pot loudly) that aren't growing!

DARLENE: What kind of bulbs?

KIM: Tulips. I followed the directions. I gave them water. Why aren't they growing?

DARLENE: When did you plant them?

KIM: Last week. Can you believe a whole week and nothing's growing? I want my money back. They said guaranteed to grow.

DARLENE: Don't tulips come up in the spring?

KIM: Then why do you plant them in the fall?

DARLENE: 'Cause they need time to grow.

KIM: But 6 months? That's ridiculous… I need them for tomorrow. I wanted the porch to look nice for Adam's party.

DARLENE: Maybe we should get some chrysanthemums while we're out.

KIM: But I wanted tulips.

DARLENE: And you will probably have them (Pause) for Easter.

KIM (Groans): Ohhhh!

DARLENE: It'll be fine. Really. Just calm down.

KIM: My in-laws are flying in for this. I need everything to be perfect. I want it to be special.

DARLENE: And it will be. First birthday parties always are.

KIM: My baby's one year old!

DARLENE: Well that makes a first birthday party appropriate then.

KIM: How come things you want to keep small grow overnight and things you need to blossom tomorrow take till spring?

DARLENE: And things you want to get into the car to go shopping won't get off the porch?

KIM: I just hate to leave when he's crying. He doesn't understand that I'll be right back.

DARLENE: But that doesn't mean you won't come back, just 'cause he doesn't understand. And just 'cause we don't know how flowers grow doesn't mean they won't eventually blossom, and just because the mall closes at 9:30 doesn't mean we have to wait till tonight to go shopping. Come on.

KIM: Hey, hey, wait a minute.

DARLENE: I've already waited several…

KIM: Shhh. Listen, he stopped crying.

DARLENE: Oh good. Now you can go and not worry the whole time. [Starts exiting through audience]

KIM: [Catching up with Darlene] Well, how do you like that? Leave him for a few minutes and he doesn't care that I've gone.

DARLENE: That's what you wanted, right?

KIM: He's probably happier with Melissa.

DARLENE: He stopped crying.

KIM: I bet he forgets who I am.

DARLENE: I seriously doubt that.

KIM: All those hours in labor and I've been replaced by a babysitter.

DARLENE: We have GOT to get you out more.

[BLACKOUT]

"Winter is Gone"

Nothing can grow without rain from God's Spirit. Nothing can bloom without Life-giving Light. Together they arc through the clouds like a promise, leading to treasure once hidden from sight.

Like blooms in the making, dreams are awakening, daring to stretch tender roots in the sod. God's Light is calling, love gently falling, bringing to Life every promise of God.

God has been watering that hidden treasure planted by Him in your heart long ago. Winter is past and the life that was promised is breaking through ground that's been softened by snow.

*Like blooms in the making, dreams are awakening, daring to stretch tender roots
in the sod. God's Light is calling, love gently falling, bringing to Life
every promise of God.*

*Arise, shine, for your Light has come. Sown by the Father,
kissed by the Son. His glory rises upon you like dawn.
It's a season of singing. The winter is gone*

We've been through some extremely long winters, but none felt longer than the two that snuck up on us when we were under construction. We lived through three major home renovations over the years due to needing more space for a growing family and updating the efficiency of our home. Twice construction started in the early fall and extended unintentionally into the winter, the long, long winter.

Renovating a kitchen or bathroom has to be the most stressful. Doing them at the same time can throw your whole world into survival mode. It's like tenting in the rain for a week and you can't wait to go home and then realize, you ARE home! UGH! Mid-project, when there's no turning back, you wonder whose brilliant idea it was and you start questioning your own sanity 'cause, yup… it was yours. And somehow after the nightmare of wintertime construction (with the constant noise, the sawdust trapped inside because it's too cold to open the windows, or worse — the horse-hair plaster that fills every crevice and covers surfaces you didn't even know existed, and whatever the estimate was, triple it, and the projected time frame? What's a time frame?) years later, you go and do it again. How soon we forget. But mid project you think, "Nothing could be worth this! I liked it better the way it was. At least we had running water. I think I wanna go back to Egypt now." Ah, the familiarity of captivity, of being confined, the coziness of claustrophobia, it takes many different forms.

Much of my life has been shaped by other people's ideas, their beliefs, their opinions and even their fears. How I see myself has been very much affected by how others perceive me or how I think others are perceiving me. Put a people-pleaser/performer in the performing arts and you can create the perfect storm, one that can easily end in a shipwreck. So here I swim, holding onto a piece of driftwood, pointing to the rest of me floating in pieces on the waves of criticism and rejection and thinking, "Um, God? Can you please do something with this?" And He says to me:

> I can and I will. But first come back to the heart of your dream. Look at the border of the puzzle. The foundation. What did you do as a kid? How were you wired before life and circumstances elbowed you off the table onto the floor in pieces? Operate in your gifts. The dream may not have manifested yet, but the gifts it will take to make it come together can be stretched and exercised each day in all you do, while you wait. Turn off the flowing undercurrent of having to make it happen (or make it look like it's happening). Live in the moment and practice your passion. I'm bringing you back to what I designed you to do. All those pieces you're holding up to Me are about to be rearranged to stronger than ever.

Winter in New England is a time that the root systems of the trees can actually expand, searching harder for moisture and nutrients because of the frozen ground. While the barren branches above look desolate and unproductive, the root system below is developing, strengthening, and advancing to support what's about to blossom. There are times God rearranges us and teaches us without us knowing we're in the middle of learning something. He discreetly snips out all the destructive lies and outdated wiring and restores us with His higher thoughts and perfect ways. We hardly even notice what's really happening; we just wake up different.

More often, though, we are painfully aware of the reconstruction and it feels like a kitchen/bathroom at the same time renovation. It takes way too long and feels traumatically dramatic! When finally, through the mess and tears, we shake our heads, "Whose idea was this? Can we please be done now?" And the Master Carpenter replies:

> I'm doing a work in you. I know what I'm doing. Trust Me. It's going to be worth it. I know it's unnerving to live with the noise of construction — a hammer falling, a wall crashing down. It's loud and it's startling. Sometimes it's hard to breathe with the all

the dust getting stirred up. It makes you feel uneasy. But I'm expanding and remodeling and giving you more freedom to move than ever before and with a far better view. It's MY job to construct and reconstruct. Your job is to be patient. Then, when it's time, you can decorate. When I'm done with you, you'll sound just like those people on TV when they have the unveiling of their newly reconstructed home. But unlike them, you really WILL be talking to Me when you say, "Oh my God, I can't believe it!"

God, I have to grin at Your sweet surprises (like completely forgotten tulips springing up after being planted half dead from the Easter before). You love to surprise us, don't You — to set us up for those really-that's-incredible moments! Like Mary at the graveside that Easter morning as she turned to see who spoke her name, it was as if you said, "Surprise, it's Me." It makes You chuckle to see us delighted, and I love to see You chuckle. It strengthens me.

If we were writing the story, it would be nothing but blue skies from now on. We associate blue skies with easy times, comfortable, pleasant and positive. But blue skies actually hide the entire universe from our sight. We can only see worlds beyond us when it's extremely dark. It takes the very things we're instinctively afraid of — the dark, the unknown, the unfathomable — to bring us to a place of revelation, awe and discernment, enabling us to truly distinguish light from darkness and to see for ourselves that the scary shadow is much larger than the actual shadow caster. "Even though I walk thru the valley of the shadow of death I will fear no evil…" (Psalm 23:4).

Jesus, how can You show Yourself faithful if there's no conflict? How can You show Yourself Light if there's no dark valley? You walked through it all first, so You could lead us through it with compassion and expertise. There was such tragedy in Your young life. You were seen as illegitimate. The government tried to kill You before You were two years old. Your step-father died and left you responsible to support Your mother and help raise Your siblings, only to have them reject You. They thought You were crazy. Your cousin was beheaded because of You. You were so misunderstood. The very mission You were on, to bring hope, life and salvation, brought rejection, torture and death, even to Your followers. But You overcame! And we shall overcome by Your Blood and by the word of our testimony (see Revelation 12:11). The gravity of a situation no longer has power over us.

Wasn't it so fun as a kid (Okay, so sometimes even now, I admit it) to hang your head upside down over the edge of the bed, so the ceiling looks like the floor and the floor looks like the ceiling and the furniture is suspended magically and the light is standing up on top of the chain that it usually hangs from? I think we were created to walk on the ceiling — to do the impossible. It feels like Jesus turned us back upside down to empty out old thinking and then sealed in the anti-gravity matter of His truth. And we can't be pulled down or have any of it fall out because His awesome truth and amazing love are sealed in us with the fire of His Spirit — melted, melded, transformed thinking, restored, renewed mind and heart. We see what everybody else sees, but we were created to walk on the ceiling, so they're really the ones seeing it upside down and telling us that what we're doing is impossible. But we're doing it... every day. It takes some major reconstruction and knocking down of walls, often times dramatic (if not traumatic) to see ourselves and the world around us the way God intended — the way He sees us, the way He loves us.

Now when it comes to how much God loves us, I can really dish it out with the best of them. I've heard it my whole life. I'm pretty sure "Jesus Loves Me" (this I know) was the first song I learned, probably before "ABCD" or maybe even before I could talk. It was not for lack of hearing that He loved me, and I truly believed that He did, but I just had a hard time receiving it, if that makes any sense. And the more I talk to people, the more I hear I'm not alone. Long time followers of Jesus (all preaching, "For God so loved the world, We love God because He first loved us, Greater love has no man than to lay down His life for his friends") were, like me, all having a hard time "feeling" His love, really receiving it. I know love can be a verb and God's love is way more than a feeling (God IS Love, for crying out loud) but for me, receiving His love means having a tangible experience, a feeling, a deep knowing. I had listened to well-known preachers sharing how in love they are with God and talking about being immersed in His love and how we can't really love God until we truly experience His love for us. I said, "God, I want that. But what's in the way here? Is it pride? Lack of trust? Whatever the wall is, please break it down. Redeem my life from the pit and crown me with love and compassion like you promised (see Psalm 103:4). You always keep Your promises. I want to receive Your love, not just believe in it."

Demolition day was about to begin with a small crack and a glimpse of His Light playfully making its way through the wall. He reminded me about the noise of reconstruction and not to be alarmed. Also, that it was my idea and if I really meant it, I needed to just be still and know that He is God.

Arise, shine, for Your Light has come. Sown by the Father, kissed by the Son. His Glory rises upon you like dawn. It's a season of singing. The winter is gone.

Chapter 3: A Tough Row to Hoe /RECEIVING LOVE

SCENE: A small girl, standing in her yard, holding a package of cucumber seeds and looking back over her shoulder.

[LIGHTS UP]

Oh goodie. He didn't follow me. That means I get to plant my own garden all by myself. I have seeds left over from my preschool fun'raiser and Daddy said we could plant them together, but I decided I will plant them all by myself and prove that I'm almost five and I'm very grown up for my age, and I can do this... I think. Planting a garden can't be too hard, can it? Maybe I should wait for Daddy. No, he's too busy with my baby brother right now. You know what? I think Daddy gets mixed up sometimes and thinks I'm still a baby too, 'cause he follows me around to see if I need help. But I'm a BIG girl and big girls can do things by themselves without any help, right? Right.

So, I'm gonna plant my own garden all by myself, 'cause I know how anyway. Dig a hole, put in the seeds, give them water, watch them grow! I remember from school 'cause we planted "merry golds" in, um, paper cups. It was fun. How much harder could this be? First you dig a little hole with your pointer finger in the nice soft dirt. [Presses on ground] The dirt in the cups was a lot softer than this. This dirt is really hard! Maybe if I use thumb man. [Tries with thumb] Ooo, I think I need Daddy to help me. What am I saying? I'm practically grown up. I can do this by myself. [Tries again] Ough! Maybe I don't need to dig a hole. I'll just put the seeds on top of the dirt. They'll get more water that way. [Tries to open package] Mmph! I can't open this. (Calls) DA... (Catches herself) No! I'm not gonna ask for help, I don't need help. I can plant them all by myself. What am I planting anyhow? [Looks at package] Cucumbers! I love cucumbers! Boy, this is gonna be great. Lots and lots of cucumbers that I grew myself. A whole garden full. [Tries again] If I could only open this package. Does it tell how to open this thing? Doesn't matter 'cause I can't read anyhow. Wow, there's lots of writing on here. I bet they're directions. Teacher says gotta follow directions. But I can't read! (Pause) Daddy can read.

You know, Daddy was really looking forward to helping me plant this garden and he's a REAL gardener. I bet he can even dig holes. I know He could open this package for me at least. He loves to help me.

You know, I think sometimes it's more grown up to ask for help. And I'm very grown up for my age. (Exiting) Daddy? Could you please help me?

[BLACKOUT]

There I sat, being still in my recliner, picturing Jesus sitting in the chair next to me and we were just talking about life and He said to me, "Go ahead, ask Him," and He pointed up to Heaven. I knew He meant ask the Father, but what was I supposed to ask Him? Then a child-like question popped into my head. Kind of smirking, Jesus nodded, "Go ahead." So I said out loud, "Daddy can you play with me?" His answer brought me to tears. It was so clear and with such a smile in His voice, "I'd love to play with you." It sounded like He had just been waiting for me to ask. "Really?" I said. And then I was a puddle on the floor. His love had melted me into a joyful puddle of tears that I could splash in. My love language is obviously "quality time," and since He made me, He knew that. When I was done, I wrote this back to Him:

"Splashing"

I'm swimming in Your love for me, splashing in my tears,
crying through the laughter, laughing at my fears.
Your glory fills the heavens. Your Voice can calm the sea.
But here You are, my Daddy God, having fun with me.

I never knew it could be this way. You were just waiting to be asked
to play, looking for a nod so You could jump in, playing hide and seek
and letting me win. Letting me find You by hearing Your laughter.
Ending my story with love ever after.

I'm swimming in Your love for me, splashing in my tears,
crying through the laughter, laughing at my fears.
Your glory fills the heavens. Your Voice can calm the sea.
But here You are, my Daddy God, having fun with me.

I never knew I could feel this free. Being, just being who You made me to be.
It's the joy on Your face as we talk while we play and the passion I sense that
You feel when I pray, that blows me away. The thought makes me cry:
just to play with me now, You were willing to die.

I'm swimming in Your love for me, splashing in my tears,
crying through the laughter, laughing at my fears.
Your glory fills the heavens. Your Voice can calm the sea.
But here You are, my Daddy God, having fun with me.

And so began the breaking of ground, or the crumbling of the wall. I realized that my Father's Heart was to have me enjoy Him as much as He enjoyed me, but I couldn't fully do that unless I understood His intentions, my purpose, and the "why me" of it all.

The lyrics of a song I had written years before for an Easter production began to sink in: "I love you, 'cause I made you. I'm dying to help you to see, when I said, 'I so loved the world' I mean you, 'cause you mean the world to Me" (I told you I could dish it out). But why me? Why does He need me? Then it struck me. If I need more than one friend to meet the different sides of ME (like my creative side, my let's-get-serious side, my be-goofy-singing-into-soup-ladle-microphones-while-dancing-in-slippery-socks-on-a-laminate-floor side) then how many more people would God, our billion times more sparkly, too many to count faceted-sided God, need to reflect His glory back to Himself? He said to me:

You complement and reflect a facet of Me that no one else does. No one else in all of history reflects that part of Me that you reflect. That is why I made you. That's why you're still on this planet at this very moment, because I'm not done polishing you. And as much as the enemy tries to mar and destroy you, I turn it for good and make you an even better reflector of that beautiful side of Me. I made you to fit together with other people so that when you gather together there's more of Me reflecting back, like a full-length mirror instead of one little compact one. There is no one else who can take your place if you're not there. You are where you are, and are who you are, because this is right where I can use you best at this moment, or you'd be somebody else, someplace else.

Your perspective is limited, so you have to trust Mine. I've literally got a God's Eye view. I'm only letting you see what you're ready to see, but that doesn't mean that's all there is.

My ideas for your life are beyond what you can imagine, but your dreams and desires are a clue of what I have for you. Don't listen to someone else's dream thinking it should be yours or that you're lacking somehow. I'm giving you what you need to accomplish YOUR mission, no one else's. So stop comparing.

Try to be still. I'm sharpening your ability to see, but a pencil sharpener is not very comfortable for the pencil. Isn't a pencil so much easier to use and doesn't it make such nice lines when it's sharp? If it doesn't hold still in the sharpener, it just spins around and comes out dazed and dizzy and just as dull.

I know you're still spinning. The pain and disappointment of loss, loneliness and financial struggles can send you into a tailspin and it's hard to get your balance. I'm here for you to grab, but your arms are crossed trying to protect your heart from further disappointment. You're not the only one.

Tell those who are lonely not to be afraid. The blessings I have for you include someone very special, very compatible who will love you unconditionally. If that just described Me would that be so awful? When the answer is "no," you'll have all that you desire.

Now for those who are afraid because of financial lack, My faithfulness will sustain you always. Your finances are only a test — a test for you to test Me with. If things don't feel balanced, it's because you're thinking it's the other way around. Now try Me in these things and be amazed. Don't delay. You're a "giver" by My design and you need this to complete the package. You can do this! You were created for this!

I know you're feeling loss and disappointment. I hear you crying, "Where's the blessing You promised? Where's the recompense?" But everything you need, to live in the blessing, is within you. Your storehouses are filled with gold purified by the fire you have passed through. That's why you dream big. Your desires have been funded by your pain. Your capacity to hold all the treasures stored up for you has now been increased. For the treasures to flow, you have to uncross your arms and let down the protective dam you created over your heart. The very thing you meant to keep the pain of disappointment out is preventing your treasure from being released. Streams of living water from within you shall flow life into your finances, life into your relationships, life into your future, your family, your ministry. It's all there behind the dam. And every time something was stolen from you, or you got abused by life unfairly or betrayed by people you trusted and yet you kept trusting Me, pure gold refined by the fire was stored. Every time you trusted Me despite the temperature of the flames, believing in My promise that the flames will not consume you, that the rivers will not overwhelm you or sweep you away, you believed in Me and here you still are! But the dam needs to be broken for the treasures to be released back into your life. You built it. Only you can take it down. Do you want to know how?

If "dam" were an acronym it would stand for you being Disappointed At Me. I didn't heal your loved one. I didn't spare you from bankruptcy. I didn't bring that special friend back into your life... yet. Release Me from the notion that somehow I owe you, and trust My timing, My goodness, and My love for you. Then ask Me to forgive you for holding onto that, for holding it up between us, and for not trusting Me. Then the dam will spring a leak that will soon turn into a flow, and then a gush — Recompense more than you imagine!

So this time I think the project in front of me turns out to be me, not so much about writing a book. I think I'm God's project and He needed to sit me down to listen, by having me write this. Even though this is only the third chapter, this is what I'm being taught about myself and maybe this is for you too: No matter what, I'm still me. Whether you like me or not, approve or disapprove, I'm still me — loved by God, valued by my Creator, though rejected or thought ill of by anyone else, still adored and accepted by God. If a holy, righteous God loves me no matter what and forgives me for absolutely anything, who am I not to love me enough to forgive myself? Am I holier or somehow a better judge of character than God? Are you? Why would I think poorly of God's workmanship, especially since it's kinda like reading and judging the rough draft of a book that's only just getting started? Obviously, we're incomplete. He's not done with me yet, and though He is Perfection, He is not perfectionistic. He doesn't expect me to be perfect until He IS done with me. I can still appreciate a work in progress and understand that the crumpled-up pages that ended up on the floor may be filled with lots of rejected words and paragraphs that just didn't work, but the process of writing them got my story to the page that I'm on. The rewrite is always better, and God can rewrite, delete, copy, and paste over anything like it never happened.

God says, "Stop caring how other people perceive you and start enjoying how I see you. The world, the ones who don't get it yet, can't appreciate you. How can they understand when even you don't get it yet? But this is what I need you to know, even if you don't quite understand — you are loved, you are safe, precious and dear to Me.

You belong to Me. Now stop spinning and just hold onto Me. Listen to the music and follow My lead."

"It's Here I Belong"

Caught up in Your Spirit, I find myself crying.
My heart has no words so my tears sing the song.
Swaying to glory without even trying.
Like dancing with Daddy, it's here I belong.

It's here I belong, Your arm tucked around me; my feet on Your feet,
the music plays on. All fear is gone, close to Your heartbeat.
Just me and my Daddy. It's here I belong.

Caught up in the music, I hear myself trying to harmonize sweetly,
but so out of key. I'm singing the words, but feel like I'm lying.
I don't belong here so I step down to see Your faceted beauty
and radiant splendor. I fall to my knees I'm so blinded by Light.
But You lift my head and say, "I'm your Defender."
Then I see You smile and I know it's alright.

It's here I belong, Your arm tucked around me; my feet on Your feet,
the music plays on. All fear is gone, close to Your heartbeat.
Just me and my Daddy. It's here I belong.

Created on purpose to reflect Your glory.
One glorious facet reflected by me.
This is my song and this is my story.
I belong here or I wouldn't be.

Caught up in Your Spirit, I find myself crying.
My heart has no words so my tears sing the song.
Swaying to glory without even trying.
Like dancing with Daddy, it's here I belong.

Chapter 3: A Tough Row to Hoe /RECEIVING LOVE

Chapter 4: Playing Interference /LISTENING

SCENE: A small child standing in a kitchen holding a homemade "cups and string telephone" talking to her Teddy bear. Her father is in the next room and is heard throughout the sketch from offstage.

[LIGHTS UP]

LEEANN: There! I did it! My very own telephone. (To Teddy bear) I wish I had somebody to try it out with. No offense, Ted, but your voice is only in my imagination so I couldn't tell if it really works or not.

DAD [From offstage]: Who are you talking to, Honey?

LEEANN: Just my bear.

DAD: Oh, okay.

LEEANN: Daddy's too busy. He won't wanna try it... I know, I can call Tommy and see if he can come over and help me try it out. No, Ted, on the real phone. I know I'm only five but I'm not stupid. [Picks up house phone] That's funny there's no buzzing sound. (Into phone) Hello? (To Ted) There's a lady on the phone. (Into phone) How did you get there, Lady? I didn't dial you. [Listens]

Mom? (To Ted) It's not a lady, it's Mom. [Back to phone] But the phone didn't ring. Where are you? [Listens] How come the car won't start? [Listens] Yeah, he's here. He's in the living room. He's trying to fix Grampy's old stereo so the station you like will come in better. It's a surprise. [Listens] Yeah, you want to talk to him? Sure. [Listens] You're welcome. [Calls] Daddy!

DAD: [From offstage] Yeah?

LEEANN (To self): Hey wait a minute. I know how I can test my phone out. [Puts cup near receiver and brings the other cup to doorway. Tries to hand it to Dad offstage]

DAD: What is it?

LEEANN: Daddy, it's for you.

DAD: I really don't have time to talk on your phone right now. I wanna finish this before Mommy gets home.

LEEANN: But it's Mommy on the phone.

DAD: I'll talk later.

LEEANN: [Goes back to real phone] He says he'll talk later. [Listens] Okay, I'll tell him. [Brings cup back to Dad, who's still offstage.] Daddy, Mommy says it's an emergency!

DAD (Amused): An emergency, huh? Okay, I suppose I have a minute.

LEEANN: [Runs offstage with cup and string. Comes back on. Holds the second cup near the receiver] Okay, Dad say something.

DAD: What's the matter, Mommy? You having an emergency?

LEEANN (Talking loudly to the receiver while holding the cup to it): Okay, say something Mom. [Pause] Did you hear that, Dad?

DAD: Hear what?

LEEANN: What Mommy said.

DAD: No, try again.

LEEANN: Go ahead, Mom, try again. [Pause] How 'bout now?

DAD: Sorry, Leeann. I can't hear anything.

LEEANN: I can hear her just fine.

DAD: Well you should talk to her then. [Throws cup back on stage] I really want to get this fixed. Mom thinks there's nothing worse than trying to listen to a radio when it's not clear. And it's driving her crazy.

LEEANN: Mom? Daddy said I should talk to you 'cause there's nothing worse than listening to you when it's not clear and your driving is crazy. [Listens] I already told him it was an emergency [Listens] He said I should talk to you 'cause he couldn't hear you... I can hear you fine. Loud and clear.

DAD [From offstage]: Hey, I think I got it! It's coming in better already. Mom is going to be so surprised.

LEEANN: Daddy says you're gonna be surprised [Listens] Really? You got a surprise for him too? Wow! [Listens] A taxi... I'll tell him. Bye, Mommy. [Hangs up phone] Boy, Ted, my Mom and Dad sure like to surprise each other. Daddy? [Walks towards the doorway] Mom says she's gonna call the taxi, at least they'll answer her call.

DAD: I'm sorry, Leeann. I'll play with you later. Maybe when I'm done here, we can fix your phone.

LEEANN: Good, 'cause I think Mommy sounded a little angry when you couldn't hear her.

DAD: You have a really good imagination.

LEEANN: Sometimes.

DAD: Well, we'll fix your phone as soon as I finish. We wouldn't want you to miss any important calls, would we?

LEEANN: You mean like if Mommy's car wouldn't start and she needed you to come get her at the gas station where they were fixing it and you couldn't hear her and she had to call a taxi instead. You mean an important call like that?

DAD: Leeann? The phone didn't ring for real did it?

LEEANN: No, it didn't ring.

DAD: Oh good! Come here, you little telephone operator. Let's see if we can make that thing work.

LEEANN [Picking up the cups and string]: Yeah, then we can surprise Mommy with it. [As exiting] After she comes home in the taxi.

[BLACKOUT]

The idea was fascinating and it was a highly recommended science-at-home activity. It was on just about everybody's "things to do on a rainy day" list when I was a kid. I don't know about you, but those cup and string phones proved pretty disappointing to me. I know they're supposed to demonstrate something about sound if you can keep the string taut enough without actually yanking the cup out of the other person's hand. But every time we tried it, I could only kind of hear what the other person was saying and mostly because they had to talk loudly and they were standing like 10 feet away from me. Did I really need the cup and string at all? It was there to prove something. I'm not quite sure exactly what, except that the real thing at the time (a highly sophisticated microphone and speaker called a receiver, attached by a curly cord to a box on the wall with fancy colorfully coated wires which were magically attached to cables outside that ran from telephone pole to telephone pole) worked a whole lot better than a string and two paper cups. You didn't even have to stand in the same room to hear the other person. I didn't need to understand how it worked in order to take advantage of it as long as I could make my little fingers turn the rotary dial to match the number I was dialing.

Too much analysis can just become frustrating and feel like a waste of time, even on a rainy day.

So, I don't want to over-analyze or beat a dead horse, but when you've been thrown off and all you want to do is beat the horse that threw you, not only can we have a hard time receiving God's love, but hearing His voice can become challenging, if not impossible at times — worse than listening through two cups and a string.

Have you ever heard yourself ask, "How come I used to hear God's voice all the time? Now all of a sudden, as hard as I try, I hear nothing. What's going on?" I'm glad you asked. So many of us ask the same thing. What's really playing interference?

When we misinterpret our difficulties as punishment from God and view our trials and suffering as discipline from an angry Bolts of Lightning Avenger striking down anybody who makes a mistake, the Voice of God starts to sound to us like, "Take that and that!" [Clap of thunder] "Maybe you'll think twice before pulling a stunt like that again!" [Crash] Having that kind of view of Him explains why so many of us have a hard time believing He's the Loving Father that He really is. We're so sin-conscious we feel unworthy and believe He must be mad at us all the time. We think that's why we can't hear Him. He's so mad He stopped talking.

If you're wounded and you're angry or disappointed with God, so you think He must feel the same way, He understands. He is not angry or disappointed with you and He's not giving you the cold shoulder. It's just hard to hear His voice if you're not ready to. Again, like in Chapter 3, release any resentment toward Him, ask His forgiveness for holding it against Him this long, and receive His love.

Sometimes we think if life treats us this poorly, God better make up for it somehow, so it's easy to feel disappointed and get angry when our demands aren't met. We have to remember the truth that God owes us NOTHING and we owe Him EVERYTHING! Our sense of entitlement is straight from satan, the father of lies, and is the lowest form of twisted thinking. It raises us above our Creator and we expect our wishes to be granted (prayers to be answered) according to our demands and in an acceptable time frame. Have you fallen into that trap? Especially if you're trying to recover from being blind-sided, your mind is apt to go straight to "Why did God let this happen again? This is so unfair!" But knowing that God is holy and just, you convince yourself, "I must be doing something wrong and He's punishing me." And even though you can't think of anything at the moment, you figure you have to be doing something wrong for all this bad stuff to keep happening.

What many of us do, instead of being angry with God, is turn our anger inward, feeling shameful for only God knows what. Inward anger leads to depression and our attempts to crawl out of it by redirecting our anger back toward God often leads us to, "How could a loving God let me suffer like this? Maybe He's not so loving or maybe He just doesn't love ME." Then we get to the place of, "Never mind Him not talking to me, I'm just not going to talk to Him anymore! He doesn't seem to hear me anyhow!" Sound familiar?

I'm so grateful God's Word includes Psalm 88, the desperate prayer of an anointed servant who, unlike most psalmists, never "gets to the good part." Heman the Ezrahite, near death and sickly most of his life, cries out to God and feels unheard, rejected, then ends his very depressing woe-is-me song with, "the darkness is my closest friend." We all have moments like Heman when it feels like God is ignoring us. The rest of Scripture assures us otherwise, but the fact that God included Psalm 88 in His Word proves that He did in fact hear Heman and cared enough to record it. By including it, God says to me:

> You might have seasons when you feel like this, but I would never inflict sickness or punish you when Jesus already took your punishment and bore your diseases. That would be double jeopardy. I AM perfectly Holy. I cannot do anything that isn't completely fair and just. I invented justice, remember? You may not see it with your own eyes, but know that I will make sure justice happens. If the devil has caused you pain or loss in any way, he will be paying for it eternally. In the meantime, I will discipline his agent, heal you of that pain if you give it to Me, and I will restore what the locusts have eaten and bring you back to health (see

Deuteronomy 32:35, Joel 2:25). If it feels to you like I'm a thousand miles away, trust My promise and not your feelings. I will NEVER leave you nor forsake you.

The storms of trauma, illness, or offense can leave a door open to all kinds of tormenting thoughts and feelings. But spirits of fear and unforgiveness can be ushered out of our lives when we recognize them and renounce the lies behind the fears, release the offender off our hook (putting them on God's hook to deal with), and trust that God will defend, avenge, and protect us. Redirect your anger at the real source — not you, and not God. God is on your side. And not the person through whom the offense came. Release them into God's Hands to bless and heal, too. That's the best way you can make the real source, the devil, regret messing with you. Then close the door by declaring the Blood of Jesus is your righteousness. Declare, "I am the righteousness of God in Christ" (see 2 Corinthians 5:21).

I know on paper I made it seem easy-breezy. I'm not trying to trivialize your pain in any way. But no matter how deep your woundedness may be, these principles stay the same. Often, we need help and guidance from a trusted friend or counselor to walk us through to freedom. My prayer writing this, is to give you hope.

If you're new in your relationship with Jesus, you're probably hearing Him more clearly than you think. Jesus said that He is the Good Shepherd and His sheep know His voice (John 4:10). If you know Jesus, you already know His voice. He called you by name and you followed because you heard Him. He warns us of an imposter (the thief) who will try to mimic Him, and so it's important to read the Bible and get used to hearing what Jesus typically says. When the Holy Spirit is guiding you, you'll understand the Bible like never before.

As time goes by and you become really familiar with what God's voice sounds like, He may turn the volume down on you a bit to teach you how to listen more intently. Like with a good friend telling you a secret, you'll get to know what His whisper sounds like. You can know when it's God because His Words will bring peace, not confusion, and

Scripture will affirm it. If you want to hear the Shepherd's voice, little sheep, just stop bleating for a minute, read His Word and listen.

So maybe you're not at all thrown off by anything in your life right now. You're still riding high up on that horse with nothing interfering that you can pinpoint. You're a seasoned listener and now, for no apparent reason, suddenly there's silence. One of the best ways to get a listener's attention while talking is to suddenly...... pause. The anticipation naturally draws them in. God may just be trying to get your attention, to draw you closer because what He's about to say is too important for you to miss. So, stop trying to guess by finishing His sentence for Him. Just lean in and get ready to hear something amazing.

Okay now, "he who has ears to hear," what else could be affecting your listening skills? There are different levels of listening depending on your relationship with the speaker or the importance of the topic to you, and if you will or won't be quizzed on it later.

Chatting and listening to the cashier at the market is going to be a tad less intense than say, listening to your teenage daughter talking about her first crush. Listening to the instructor teaching you how to open your parachute may hold your attention a bit more closely than the salesperson at the kiosk explaining why you need to buy "Wonderall Miracle Cream" before it's too late.

When I'm in conversation with someone whose expertise is beyond me, I half-listen when they're talking because I'm trying so hard to come up with something intelligent to say before it's my turn to talk. I nod like I'm really listening and hope they don't ask me a question. I don't want to appear as stupid as I feel. In a similar way, when we're young or immature we're not the best listeners because we're working so hard to formulate our own ideas and opinions. We simply don't have the reference points or experience to relate to the more mature speaker and it makes us feel like everyone in the whole world obviously knows more than us. We try to compensate by convincing ourselves, and everybody else (with the toss of our head and a roll of our eyes) that we, in fact, know everything. As much as we want to hear ourselves say our new ideas out loud and try them on for size to see how they sound, and even though there's an urgency to be heard and valued by those older and wiser, it's much less intimidating bouncing them off peers or those younger than us. That's why we tend to avoid talking and listening to adults if we don't have to. There's less of a chance of having our tender ideas challenged that way.

Mature people (of all ages) usually have an easier time listening. We've learned to encourage other people's ideas, even learn from them, and only gently suggest or add to them when asked our opinion. By now we have many opinions, to be sure, and we have life experience to back them up. In general, at this point we don't have the same need to hear ourselves talk (we just write a book instead). We also tend to be less busy and hopefully we've learned people are more important than productivity. We've grown to especially value the stories and opinions of those ahead of us. Like panning for gold, we can actually benefit and enjoy listening to them recount and embellish tales of yore. We can listen without trying to correct them or impress them with our "vast knowledge." Most mature people realize that the more we know, the more we know how much we DON'T know.

So how well you listen and hear God's voice will greatly depend on your relationship with Him, your humility, your maturity, and how important what He says really is to you.

We're designed to hear Him if we choose to pay attention. Take note of your most comfortable learning style (kinesthetic, auditory, visual, verbal, etc.) and you'll probably discover your easiest "listening-to-God-speak-to-you" style. For me, kinesthetic as I am, whenever I'm trying to take in information, I find myself tapping my fingers, twiddling my thumbs or stroking a cat or something soft as I listen or read. Even now, as I listen for what to write next, I'm rubbing my hands together. I know people who have to have music blasting to focus on assignments or projects. Noise in the background helps them create, write, and process. I, on the other hand, am so audibly distracted that to focus on directions while I'm driving or to get across a busy intersection, I have to turn the music off and insist on silence from any passengers.

Of course, there are so many combinations of learning/listening styles that we're all going to have our own best ways to hear God, and there really isn't one superior to another. But I believe there is one we probably have in common. We were created by the vibrations of God's voice. Words will vibrate change whether we read, write, say, listen to, or think them. They carry ideas, feelings, and messages. Verbal learning, I believe, is across the board part of everyone's "listening for God's Voice" skill set. Hearing or reading God's Word is primary. But no matter our language or reading level, our Awesome Creator God, best of all teachers, designed His creation to speak to all of us and teach us at every level, every listening style:

> The heavens declare the glory of God; the skies proclaim the work of his hands. Day after day they pour forth speech; night after night they display knowledge. There is no speech or language where their voice is not heard. Their voice goes out into all the earth, their words to the ends of the world (Psalm 19:1-4).

So, like the couple in this next story with a life decision to make, if you need to hear from God, maybe you should just go camping:

"Now You're Talkin'"

SCENE: Stage set like a campsite at night. Frank, with an unmade tent on the ground in front of him, is looking at directions with a flashlight.

[LIGHTS UP DIMLY]

DOLORES [From offstage]: Frank? Franklin? FRANKLIN!

FRANKLIN: What is it now Dolores? I'm busy.

DOLORES: Would you please shine that flashlight over here before I kill myself trying to find my way back.

FRANKLIN: If I shine the light over there then I won't be able to see these directions of how to put up our brand new, super deluxe King Elvis Goes Camping Tent. [Shines light on tent] Ain't she a beauty, Dolores?

DOLORES: Shine the flashlight over here Frank or I'll light a match to that tent of yours so I can see where the heck I'm going.

FRANKLIN: All right Dolores, you don't hafta get so huffy… Here. [Shines light]

DOLORES [Enters]: I can't believe you went and forgot the kerosene for our lantern.

FRANKLIN: I remembered the flashlight, didn't I?

DOLORES: That's the flashlight I keep in the glove compartment for emergencies.

FRANKLIN: But I remembered it was there.

DOLORES: Frank, I just don't understand why we can't check into a motel tonight and set up tomorrow [Thunder] in the sunshine, was that thunder?

FRANKLIN: No, just a truck on the highway.

DOLORES: We are miles from any highway. Oh Frank, the boys are sleeping all crunched up in the back seat. Can't we just go to a motel for tonight? And stop shinin' that thing in my face.

FRANKLIN: [Shuts off flashlight] I am not staying in any motel when we could be sleeping in our brand new, super deluxe King Elvis Goes Campin' Tent. Soon as we get it set up, we can move the boys inside. They'll sleep better in this tent than in any motel room. Now come on. This tent goes up in a jiffy. [Hands her directions and flashlight] You read me the directions, I'll put it up.

[Dolores can't get the flashlight on.]

FRANKLIN: Come on Dolores. What's it say?

DOLORES: It says, "Before setting up this tent in the dark make sure the batteries in your flashlight are workin'." Frank, the flashlight just died. Can we please go to a...

FRANKLIN: No motel, Dolores. We'll use the headlights of the car.

DOLORES: The car's parked way down in the gully. The lights won't reach up here.

FRANKLIN: Well... we won't use directions then. How difficult could it be? The salesman said it was a snap.

DOLORES: We should call him up here to do it then. You can't set up a tent you've never set up before with no directions in the dark [Rain starts] and IN THE RAIN. Come on, Frank. Roll it back up and let's get out of here. [Uses directions for head cover]

FRANKLIN: Nothin doin', Dolores. I came out here with my brand new, super deluxe King Elvis Goes Campin' Tent and I'm not wasting a whole night someplace else. I'm staying right here. Remember why we came campin' in the first place?

DOLORES: I keep asking myself that.

FRANKLIN: So we could be near nature. It was your idea. You said it would help us get some perspective, remember? [Crawls into unmade tent as is]

DOLORES: Oh yeah, I did say that, didn't I. [Notices Frank in the tent] Franklin Terwilliger, what are you doing?

FRANKLIN: Staying dry. It's raining out there.

DOLORES (Sarcastically): Oh really, I hadn't noticed. Why don't we just go sit in the car?

FRANKLIN: A real man never abandons his tent. It's not so bad in here, Dolores, you should try it.

DOLORES: I'm not coming in there, but I can't very well talk to you like this. Would you please come out here?

FRANKLIN: And get soakin' wet? Not me.

DOLORES: But this is important, Frank. Remember why we came up here?

FRANKLIN: I just reminded you, remember?

DOLORES: We came up here because we have some really important decisions to make.

FRANKLIN: Tell me about it.

DOLORES: They could be life-changing.

FRANKLIN: I know that. That's why I don't wanna make them.

DOLORES: Frank, I can't talk to you like this.

FRANKLIN: Then don't.

DOLORES: But we need to talk. (Sighs and resigns) Oh, why not? [Crawls in] Hey, it's not bad in here.

FRANKLIN: Told you.

DOLORES: Frank, we can't stay here tonight. You know that don't you?

FRANKLIN: Why not? I like it here.

DOLORES: Sometimes you gotta hear what circumstances are shoutin' at you.

FRANKLIN: I don't hear anything.

DOLORES: I know you don't Frank. You often don't. That's why I thought if we came up here camping it would help you listen better to what God is tryin' to tell you.

FRANKLIN: How is campin' gonna help?

DOLORES: You know Frank, making life-changing decisions is kinda like setting up a tent.

FRANKLIN: Say what?

DOLORES: We hafta read the directions, in the light of day, and listen to the circumstances and talk to people who know about such things. We can't just stumble around in the dark or stand in an unmade tent because we like it here in the pourin' rain. Don't you see? God knows our future. That's why I wanted us to be here, closer to nature, so we could have time to get closer to God and listen to what He's sayin'.

FRANKLIN: Yeah and what's He sayin' now, Dolores?

DOLORES: Go to a motel, Frank. He's sayin' go to a motel.

FRANKLIN: I suppose we shouldn't argue with Him, huh?

DOLORES: Now you're talkin', Frank… or I should say, now you're listenin'.

FRANKLIN: No, Dolores. I hafta go. [Emerging from the tent]

DOLORES: Because you feel it's the wise thing to do. [Emerges]

FRANKLIN: No, because I didn't bother stopping at the rest area before we got here. I hafta go. [Exits]

DOLORES: Oh… well, I guess God knows what it takes to get us where He wants us to go.

FRANKLIN: Come on Dolores. Hurry up!

DOLORES: What about the… [Points to the tent]

FRANKLIN: You said He's telling us to go to a motel, now let's go.

DOLORES [Looking up and smiling]: Whatever you say.

[BLACKOUT]

Isn't it frustrating when you go on a road trip and your favorite listening-stations, that you have so nicely preset on your car radio, one by one turn to static? You're down to the last audible favorite station and frantically are trying to tune it. You hear a faint echo of what might possibly be your favorite song, but you can't tell through all the crackling and annoying buzzes, when suddenly... just static! Aaah! Nothing changed with the signal from the station and your receiver's not damaged. You're just out of range. So you set your radio to scan and the only station that does come in, and of course obnoxiously loudly, clear as a bell, is your least favorite kind of music and/or an "all talk all the time" station. All you really want and need is YOUR music. There are times we wander away a bit too far from what God is broadcasting to us and all we hear instead is static or the wrong station.

If not hearing God's voice is like you being out of range, having technical difficulties due to a storm, maybe not being sure of your favorite station yet, or possibly it's dead airspace, then God may be trying to communicate with you in a different way than you're used to. This could be a time when He wants to expand your listening skills by redesigning or repositioning your receiver. He could be taking you to a whole new level of listening. Like a wink, nod or nudge from a loved one can signal you into action, no words necessary, listening for the Holy Spirit's prompting will become even more intimate during these silent times.

If you're not hearing from God at the moment and you want to be, three things I find very helpful and restorative no matter how damaged or distanced I might feel are: the beauty and message of nature (to all our senses), the comforting truth of God's Word (especially the Psalms), and praying in the Spirit (to minister to heart and soul). Let your other senses take over for a while and see, smell, taste, feel, and hear what happens. And remember, you may not be hearing God's Voice at the moment, but you're still experiencing His grace. Surely Jesus is with you always, to the very end of the age (see Matthew 28:20).

I saved one of the biggest interferences, for most of us, for last. Can you guess what it is?

Have you ever tried to share your heart with someone who insisted on doing something else while they listened? Did you feel heard? Maybe you did. Maybe your listening style includes moving or doodling or taking notes, so you get it. But I'm talking about if someone is not paying full attention to what you're saying because they're multitasking or half-listening. There's something to be said for undivided attention. What a difference when someone says, "Hold my calls. Shut the door. Let's sit down. I want to hear what you've got to say." It makes you feel valued and important, no matter what your listening style happens to be.

You may not be a verbal listener, you may not even like to read, but if you wanted to get to know me better, you could read this book and find out more about me, what I think, how I view life. You may even find out that we're a lot alike or possibly completely opposite. But if you're reading this now, it's an indication that you think there is some value to what I have to say, even if that value is finding something with which to contrast your ideas and opinions. If you read this book cover to cover or just five minutes here and there, the act of choosing to read shows you value it somehow. So, thank you.

If there was a best seller of all time, full of stories, letters and accounts of supernatural encounters people have had with the living God since the beginning of recorded time, and it contained ancient records of historical events teaching us what to do and not to do so we can learn from others' mistakes and be spared needless suffering; if it had chapters of instructions, principles to live by and wisdom recorded by Solomon himself: ancient writings preserved to benefit future generations, teaching and transforming them, would you want to at least look at it?

Focusing on the Words of God written down for us over the centuries and giving them our full attention for even five minutes would show we somewhat value what God has to say.

I believe reading or listening to God's letter to us is life-giving and supernaturally, unexplainably essential to our sense of well-being. It's the most read book of all time. So how come it takes so much discipline and effort to read the Bible? Could it be that some of us have been "encouraged" a bit too forcefully (guilted into it) and now it feels too much like required reading? Or maybe it's just the opposite.

For hundreds of years it was actually discouraged by those in church leadership for laymen to read the Bible without a priest to interpret what it meant. It was presented as mysterious and dangerous and those who read it on their own were made to feel guilty, fearful or ashamed. Is that affecting you?

What else (or who else) could be playing interference?

The thief (the devil) comes to steal, kill and destroy. Whatever schemes or arrows are being flung at you by the thief, God's Word (whether read, heard, dreamed, or envisioned) can remedy. Of course all kinds of interference would come against you to try to keep you from getting a hold of the counter-strategy that restores and enables you to stand or take back ground. But the devil, though he plays a definite part, is not the biggest interference with hearing God's voice.

Have you figured out what it is? I'll give you a hint: It's something that belongs to you and you can choose to spend it, take it, or waste it. To hear God's voice, we need to be willing to take and spend it. It's your time. Spending time with God, taking time to really listen, shows you value hearing from Him more than anything else at that moment.

You may need it quiet. You may need music blasting. You may need to drive, walk, sing, or dance. However God created you, it takes time, spending time, to really listen. You may need to pat a cat, tap your fingers, go camping, or write a book, but what you really need to hear God's voice most of all, I think, is just time.

It's time to give God your full attention the way you listen best or the new way He's teaching you. Whatever style that it happens to be and however you want to word it, it's time to say, "Hold my calls. Shut the door. Let's sit down. I want to hear what You've got to say."

"Speak, Lord, for your servant is listening" (1 Samuel 3:10).

Chapter 4: Playing Interference /LISTENING

Chapter 5: A Clean Sweep /OBEDIENCE

SCENE: A cluttered living room with a door (stage right) that leads to the front porch, and a door (stage left) to the TV room.

[LIGHTS UP]

[Wife is vacuuming the living room. Husband walks in and taps her on the shoulder and she jumps.]

WIFE: Ohhh! Don't do that! [Shuts off vacuum]

HUSBAND (Half laughing): I'm sorry. I didn't mean it.

WIFE: Yeah, getting your jollies making me lose it, first thing in the morning.

HUSBAND: I just wanted to say, "Happy Birthday!"

WIFE: Well, now you're gonna have to add about ten more candles to my cake. Scare me half to death.

HUSBAND: I got you a surprise.

WIFE: I've had enough surprises, thank you.

HUSBAND (Temptingly): You're gonna love it.

WIFE (Curious): Where is it?

HUSBAND: She'll be here any minute.

WIFE: Who?

HUSBAND: Are you ready for this?

WIFE: I don't think so.

HUSBAND: I hired you a maid for a day.

WIFE: You what?

HUSBAND: She's coming at 9:00. So put the vacuum cleaner away. Make yourself a cup of tea, grab a good book, and sit down. [Sits her down and moves footstool over] Here put your feet up and enjoy your day off. I have to call some clients. I'll be in my office. (As exiting) Happy Birthday!

WIFE: Yeah, thanks. Wow, a maid... coming here? [Jumps up] I gotta get this place picked up! [Furiously fast background music plays as she frantically stashes clutter, especially into the TV room offstage, newspapers under the couch cushion, etc.]

[Music stops. Knock on the door]

WIFE (Whimpers): Ahhh! She's here. [Straightens herself and opens the door] Hi.

MAID: Mrs. Newhardt?

WIFE: Mm-hmph.

MAID: Hello, I'm Carl, from Clean Sweep. Happy Birthday.

WIFE: You're a man.

MAID: I know.

WIFE: I'm sorry, I was just expecting... never mind. Come on in. As you can see I don't think I really need a maid so...

MAID: We at Clean Sweep know that today's busy homeowner needs a break once in a while, an extra hand to help tidy things up when life gets too hectic.

WIFE: Well, I think I do a pretty good job keeping my house in order. I really don't think a maid is necessary, no offense. Maybe the garage. That's my husband's domain. It's always a mess.

MAID: Well, I've been hired to clean your house and I'm prepared for housework. [Looking around] Isn't there some corner or closet that could use some straightening? We all have those places to stash things when unexpected company is popping over. [Pulls out the stashed newspaper from under the cushion] I'd like to help you get them in order, so you won't have to worry about it.

WIFE: [Grabbing newspaper] My corners are fine, thank you. Why don't you… take the day off.

MAID: I really can't do that. Your husband has already paid for me to clean the house. Can't I just vacuum for you or at least dust? I know how tedious dusting can get, especially if you're not being paid to do it.

WIFE: No, I don't…

MAID: It IS your birthday.

WIFE: That's true, it is. (Pause) Well, okay, you can vacuum.

MAID: Great! Do you have a vacuum cleaner or would you like me to use mine?

WIFE: Of course I have a vacuum cleaner.

MAID: Oh good… and where do you keep it?

WIFE (Nervously): Oh, it's in the TV room, right now.

MAID: Fine, I'll just start in the TV room. And where is that?

WIFE (Guarding door with her life): I just cleaned in there, that's why the vacuum cleaner is in there so I'll get the vacuum cleaner for you, okay? [Opens door a crack and sneaks into room.]

[Maid smiles knowingly.]

WIFE: [Enters with vacuum cleaner and slams door quickly] Here you go.

MAID: Thank you. [Pause] Mrs. Newhardt, I know it's awkward having someone else come into your house to clean. Not many of us want to admit that sometimes parts of our houses get downright dirty.

WIFE: Not my house.

MAID: A lot of times we don't even notice how messy a room has gotten until company drops in or a maid comes...

WIFE: Are you suggesting...

MAID: Please understand that I'm not trying to insult you. I just want to help. I know what it's like to live a busy life. No one can expect you to keep a perfect house.

WIFE: But I can try.

MAID: It's good to try, but it's humanly impossible to be perfect. You've got life to live, and in anyone's life things are bound to get pushed under the rug or into a closet once in a while. My job, if you'll let me do it, is to clean it up. Why don't you let me clean the TV room?

WIFE [Still guarding the door]: I told you, I just cleaned it.

MAID: Mrs. Newhardt, I've seen a lot worse than what's probably in that room, but even if it wins the prize for the messiest, I want to help you get things in order.

WIFE: I can do it myself, thank you.

MAID: Sometimes it's just so overwhelming it's easier to ignore it, or put it off to another day. But today's your birthday, the first day of the rest of your life. What better way to start than with a clean slate, even the corners. And making things clean is what I do best. Please let me go in there. Trust me. You'll be so glad if you do.

WIFE: You've seen some real messes, huh?

MAID: Messier than you can imagine.

WIFE (Resigns): Um… All right then. [Steps aside]

MAID: [Opens door and looks in the room, then turns back to her] Oh, this isn't that bad. This will be easy.

WIFE: I'd feel better if I could help.

MAID: Of course, you can. That will make it even easier. We'll be done in no time. [Exits]

WIFE (To self): I guess the hardest part was opening the door.

[BLACKOUT]

Wow, I think I hit a writing wall. I've been tootling along for the last few weeks and here I am at Chapter 5 and all of a sudden… nothing. I'm trying to hear what God is saying to me and it's as if I have my fingers in my ears and I'm humming a merry little tune "la, la, la" and not hearing anything else. Maybe I should reread Chapter 4 on listening. Okay, so now I'm hearing a four-letter word. I don't really like to say it much, but it seems like that's what I'm supposed to write next. It's something I've struggled with my whole life. It starts with "O, you think?" and ends with, "but whY?" and in between sits BE: as in be-havior, be-good, be-cause I said so: O-BE-Y. Okay, so I wrote it down, but do I really have to talk about it now? I'm part of the question-authority generation. Write a chapter on obedience and that other thing? Can I even get it out? Maybe if I look the other way while I write… SUB… MI… SSION.

Honestly, I thought I could skip over this topic, but there was this sketch, and when I pulled it out and read it again, twenty years after I wrote it, I felt the same pang in my stomach as the woman in the sketch. You want me to go here again? I thought I was all done letting You into my messy rooms to clean, but obviously there's more work to do, huh?

I was a "No, I don't wanna," but then I'd go and do it, kind of kid. Required reading to me meant required skimming just enough to fake my way through the report. Don't tell me what to read. Stubborn? I like to think of me as strong-willed. Rebellious? More like an independent thinker. Dig in and don't back down? No, just tenacious. Obedient? If it sounds like a good idea and I feel like doing it, of course I'm obedient — as long as you don't tell me what to do.

When our daughter was just learning to walk and the coffee table was both an anchor for balance and a tender little forehead's worst nightmare, I remember having an ah-ha moment. Through the challenge of trying to let her learn but protect her at the same time, I realized, "This is what God must feel like all the time." I had this first born to teach me more about my relationship with Daddy God than I had learned in twenty-three years. Then, I had my second born to teach me about how incredibly patient God has to be with me and how even guardian angels can be given a run for their money.

Yes, there is definitely some satisfaction that comes seeing your adult children as parents deal with some of the same challenges they caused for you. I'm blessed to be able to see firsthand, as my husband and I live with our daughter, son-in-law, and their two boys, just how full circle really works. As if learning about my tendency to rebel and disobey didn't quite hit home enough the first time around, God is giving me an even clearer view as a grandparent. This time I can observe from a much less personally offendable position and just see myself in my grandkids, as well as my daughter, as they drive it home to me. I'm looking in a mirror everyday as I watch the delayed obedience, selective hearing, attorney-like arguments (from a ten-year-old), and the creative excuses for not following through on a parent's request. Rationalization starts very young.

My husband and I were both blessed with parents who were happily married to their spouses for over fifty years. We both had parents who were stable and trustworthy. We were also able to parent the best we could, looking to our Father God as the ultimate Authority to Whom we and our children answered. But even so, surrounded by loving parents and grandparents who loved Jesus and tried to live according to His commands, I still struggled with submission. I can only imagine how impossible to "trust and obey" sounds to those who have suffered through abuse.

But I think submission and obedience and letting someone in to clean your house all come down to the same thing — being able to trust that Someone.

My whole life God keeps asking me, "Do you trust Me?" Step by step, event by big event, relationship by relationship, "Do you trust Me?" Crisis by crisis, loss by loss, "How about now? Do you still trust Me?" Many times I answered "No" at first, and then His love would flood through my doubt and fear and the peace of "Yes, of course, I trust You," would come out through the tears. That is the submission He's looking for. It's not about submitting to His rules. God is asking us to submit to the truth of His character and goodness. He is pure Love. NOTHING ever changes that. Part of my learning to obey (and I'm still learning) came from focusing on Who He is:

You are my Joy, my Fortitude, my Righteousness, my Deliverer, Keeper, Teacher, Revealer of Mysteries, Giver of Dreams, You are God, Majesty and Goodness, Forever Faithful and True, Forever the Same, Never Changing, Always Kind, Always Gracious, Jesus, You are Love. You ARE Beauty.

Your strength poured out; Your Body broken. Each stripe took Your breath from You. Each lash ripped away my pain. By Your wounds, by Your stripes, I am healed. I am free. As You clung on the post, the whole world reeling, Your heart and head pounding, hanging there for me, excruciating pain, Flesh for flesh, buying back, redeemed and restored bodies, never ending, full of life, full of You.

You're the Hand, I'm the glove. I'm the heart, You're the Love. Spirit of Life, Gentle Dove. Full of You. You're the Oil, I'm the jar. I'm the wick, You're the Fire. Spirit of Life, Morning Star. Full of You.

He's the One holding us together and He will see us through the sweeping of a nation and the sweeping of our messy lives. He is mighty to save, slow to anger when it comes to His children. Our Abba, Daddy.

He's our Furious, Fiery Avenger, our Fierce and Perfect Lover,
Protector and Corrector, Nurturer and Friend.

That's the God we serve. That's the Creator Who serves us! How amazing and absurd is that? Jesus came to serve US! And like a loving, kind, attentive parent, He says, "If you love Me, you will obey what I command" (John 14:15).

If you've ever tried to take care of anyone or anything else, even a pet, you know the frustration of not having them cooperate with you. You could almost hear yourself say to them, "If you appreciate what I'm doing for you even a little, if you have any idea of how hard this is, please do what I ask you to do. Help me help you! Don't touch that hot stove. And don't drink the bottle of orange-flavored cough syrup off the top shelf with the child proof cap (obviously only adult proof) by pulling out drawers to make steps so you can reach, when I tell you not to. Please come when I call you so we won't miss the first inning of the game you're supposed to pitch, ya know, for that team that you begged to be on when I knew it would mean sacrificing so many of my evenings. And now you're too busy (trying to beat the next level) when I call you for the third time to get in the car, and where's your baseball cap you just had on your head two minutes ago? [All purely hypothetical of course] If you love me, if you care even a little bit about me, will you please tell me where you're going, or at least tell me THAT you're going, before taking off on your bike to the park, by yourself, again, just before supper? If you want me to keep taking care of you, for crying out loud, would you please just do what I ask you?"

Now amplify the kind of love and care that we give to those around us, about a billion times more, and you can begin to see why Jesus would say, "If you love Me, obey My commands." He's not being egotistical or dictatorial or even controlling. He simply loves us more than anything, knows what's best for us, sees the future, and is trying to direct our paths from high above this corn maze we call life. Trust in the Lord with all your heart. Don't lean on your own understanding. In all your ways acknowledge Him and He'll direct your path, He'll make your way straight (from Proverbs 3:5-6). "Trust Me," Jesus says.

"Let me into your messiest room." And here's what He means by that. Here is what He says He really wants from us:

I want your honesty more than anything — no facades, no performances, no resumes. I want all of who you are so far, with all your tender spots and weaknesses and even your selfishness. I want you to be honest with Me and with yourself.

I want you to know that nothing (no thought, mistake, method, attitude, wrongful action, failure or independent streak) will damage my plans for you or change My adoration of you. Rest in all of life's lessons so far. Don't waste time reliving them, trying to recover them, undo them, or rethink them. Stand on top of them and look ahead. No shame. I've put them under your feet so you can stand higher and see farther.

You know how you used to love that drawing game, making a picture out of somebody else's scribbled line? That's what I can do from your mistakes. I can turn your "oops" moments into something helpful and even beautiful. You don't have to fix you or anybody else. Your call is to love whoever I put in front of you to love.

Sometimes love is listening. Sometimes praying. Sometimes just speaking truth. Never is it about trying to change someone. That's judging, not loving. Love uses discernment to see who someone really is and what's clinging onto them pretending to be part of them, then dismissing what doesn't belong. Now extend that discerning love to yourself... because I have.

I know you love to decorate and pay attention to details. So do I. Details transform what's simple into what's simply amazing, and can make a picture pop off the page. I'm a God of details, and often behind-the-scene ones. Your life, and the season you're in, is a detail that makes My story, My artwork, My song, pop off your page. The smudges you make, the messes, get written over, painted over, or sung over.

I'm watching over you. I want what's best for you. You don't have to prove anything to me. I want to prove Myself to YOU. But taking care of you would be so much easier if you'd just trust Me enough to obey Me.

"Trust and Obey" written by John H. Sammis 1887

When we walk with the Lord in the Light of His Word, what a glory He sheds on our way! While we do His good will, He abides with us still, And with all who will trust and obey.

Not a shadow can rise, not a cloud in the skies, but His smile quickly drives it away; Not a doubt or a fear, not a sigh or a tear, Can abide while we trust and obey.

Not a burden we bear, not a sorrow we share, but our toil He doth richly repay; Not a grief or a loss, not a frown or a cross, But is blessed if we trust and obey.

But we never can prove the delights of His love until all on the altar we lay; For the favor He shows, for the joy He bestows, Are for them who will trust and obey.

Then in fellowship sweet we will sit at His feet, or we'll walk by His side in the way; What He says we will do, where He sends we will go; Never fear, only trust and obey.

Trust and obey, for there's no other way To be happy in Jesus, but to trust and obey.

I had a love/hate relationship with that old hymn as a child. It was a catchy tune with easy words to sing and I knew there was truth in there somewhere. But there were a few phrases that really bothered me. We usually just sang the first and the last stanzas with the chorus before, in between, and after. Let me give you the version of what my seven-year-old ears and heart thought the song said:

Trust and obey, for there's no other way
to be happy in Jesus, but to trust and obey.

[My 7-year-old interpretation: If you wanna be happy, you better obey Jesus or you're not gonna like it too much, trust me.]

When we walk with the Lord in the Light of His Word, what a
glory He sheds on our way! While we do His good will,
He abides with us still, And with all who will trust and obey.

[Interpretation: When you walk with Jesus, there's gonna be lots of bright light. As long as you obey Him and do good, He'll stay with you. If not, He's outta there and taking His light with Him.]

Then in fellowship sweet we will sit at His feet, or we'll walk by His side
in the way; What He says we will do, where He sends we will go;
Never fear, only trust and obey.

[Interpretation: Church "fellowship" always meant punch & cookies, but we gotta sit at Jesus' feet to have them, 'cause when we walk next to Him, we get in His way. When He tells you to do scary things, just do it. And you better not be afraid, 'cause He said not to be.]

Maybe I can blame some of my issues on this song. Maybe not. But even now, I'm only just beginning to understand why this song was so dear to my grandparents and the other old Swedish Baptists of my childhood church family. It's taken a lifetime of God proving His faithfulness to me over and over: through the shadows, clouds, doubts and fears, burdens, sorrow, sighs and tears, grief and loss, frowns and cross, He's shown His favor and bestowed His unexplainable joy to me time and time again.

"Who among you fears the Lord and obeys His servant? If you are walking in darkness, without a ray of light, trust in the Lord and rely on your God. For the Lord God is our light and protector. He gives us grace and glory. No good thing will the Lord withhold from those who do what is right. O Lord Almighty, happy are those who trust in You" (Isaiah 50:10, Psalm 84:11-12, *NLT*).[1]

Can you hear His voice echo in the words of this chapter's sketch:

> I know its awkward having someone else come into your house to clean. Not many of us want to admit that sometimes parts of our houses get downright dirty. A lot of times we don't even notice how messy a room has gotten until company drops in or a maid comes... Please understand that I'm not trying to insult you. I just want to help... No one can expect you to keep a perfect house. It's humanly impossible to be perfect. You've got life to live, and in anyone's life things are bound to get pushed under the rug or into a closet once in a while. My job, if you let Me do it, is to clean it up. Why don't you let Me... even if it wins the prize for messiest, I want to help you get things in order. Today's the first day of the rest of your life. What better way to start than with a clean slate? Making things clean is what I do best. Please, let Me go in there. Trust Me. You'll be so glad if you do.

Jesus is standing at the door and knocking.
Isn't it time to trust Him enough to let Him in?

---

[1] *Holy Bible*, New Living Translation, copyright© 1996. Wheaton Illinois: Tyndale House Publishers, Inc.

Chapter 6: Surprise! /PRAYER

SCENE: Person 1 is sitting center stage, staring at an unlit candle on the table in front of her. As **LIGHTS COME UP,** Person 2 sneaks onto the stage behind her. Takes off party hat (Oops) and tosses it offstage, then silently motions to the people offstage, "She's right here. I'll get her in there."

PERSON 1 (Without taking eyes off candle): What can I do for you?

PERSON 2 (Caught): How did you know I was here? I didn't say anything.

PERSON 1: I could just feel you standing there.

PERSON 2: That's too weird.

PERSON 1: Can't put much past me.

PERSON 2: I'll say. [Motions off stage "1 minute" then crosses to Person 1]

PERSON 1: So whaddya want?

PERSON 2: Um… I need your help in the other room. Could you help me for a minute?

PERSON 1: I'm kinda busy.

PERSON 2: You are? Doing what?

PERSON 1: Isn't it obvious?

PERSON 2: Um… (Clueless) Doing a science project?

PERSON 1: No. I'm waiting.

PERSON 2: Waiting for… (Expecting Person 1 to complete the sentence)

PERSON 1: For the candle to light.

PERSON 2: Want a match?

PERSON 1: No thanks. God's gonna light it.

PERSON 2 (Baffled): And why would God light the candle?

PERSON 1: I need Him to.

PERSON 2: No you don't. We have matches.

PERSON 1: I asked God to prove to me He was really here by lighting the candle.

PERSON 2: So if it doesn't light, it means He's not here?

PERSON 1: I've really gotta know that He is. I hafta see for myself.

PERSON 2: Well, I appreciate your sincerity, but your method may not be exactly effective. Just 'cause you can't see Him doesn't mean He's not here. He's like the wind…

PERSON 1: I know, I know, you can't see it, but you can feel it and see its effect on things.

PERSON 2: Right.

PERSON 1: Well, I wanna see God's effect on this candle. I wanna feel His presence. I've gotta know for sure that what I believe is the truth.

PERSON 2: The truth is, God is everywhere.

PERSON 1: Well, let Him prove it then.

PERSON 2: He proves Himself to us all the time.

PERSON 1: Good, then He'll light the candle for me.

PERSON 2: He doesn't always show us in a way that we expect Him to, but we can experience His presence if we just keep our eyes open.

PERSON 1: Well that's what I'm doing, keeping my eyes open. I'm not taking them off this candle except to pray.

[As Person 1 closes her eyes to pray, Person 3 comes around the corner and motions "Come on" to Person 2. Person 2 shrugs.]

PERSON 1: Please light the candle. If You're here please, please, please light the candle.

PERSON 2: Look, can you just come help me in the other room for ONE minute? Then you can come right back here and wait for the candle to light…

PERSON 1: Don't you understand? It's my 30th birthday. It's like a turning point in my life. I gotta know God's really here. I don't wanna miss Him!

PERSON 2: God doesn't want you to miss Him either. That's why He's so patient with us and tries again and again to show us that He really IS here, but don't stare so hard at the candle that you can't see anything else.

PERSON 1: If He really cares about me, He'll light a candle.

[Person 1 continues to stare at the candle, while others enter in party hats.]

PERSON 3: If we can't get you to the party, we'll bring the party to you.

ALL: Surprise!

[People sing "Happy Birthday" to Person 1, who is oblivious as a cake lit with candles is brought in behind her. She never turns around to see it, but just stares at the unlit candle in front of her.]

PERSON 1: [When they finish singing and still staring ahead] Can't He light just one little candle?!

[BLACKOUT]

It's funny how we get an idea in our heads of what God is like, what He's capable of, because we've had a glimpse of His power or faithfulness and then we freeze frame Him there. We like formulas, recipes, and guaranteed outcomes, so we contain Him thinking that's all there is of Him, this is as far as He'll go. He's unchanging, so we shouldn't expect any more than what we've already experienced. Besides, He's more predictable and safer that way.

How many times have we explained to God just when and how He should fix something for us, based on our limited faith in His capabilities, and ignorant of His true desires for us? We may not exactly instruct Him, but our prayers and what we ask for give us away. We half expect Him to light the candle on the table in front of us when instead He has a room full of friends and a cake full of lit candles waiting right behind us. How many miracles have we missed or not recognized because we were looking for things to be done our way — instantly, easily, and of course, painlessly?

After watching a documentary on God's extravagant creative healing miracles, in which people received, on the spot, gold teeth from Heaven (to replace broken or compromised molars), I prayed for my broken tooth with the sharp edge to be fixed. The next day the sharp edge broke off. No gold, but it was much more comfortable. Was it any less of a miracle because it wasn't what I'd call extravagant? It was an answer to prayer, and miraculous to me none the less.

SO much greater is God than we can even imagine — more generous and merciful than we ever expect. Even though I know He wants me whole and healed down to my teeth, to direct Him or try to manipulate Him by demanding my blessings be delivered a certain way is not only arrogant, but I think must sadden Him. He is way more powerful and probably has so much more to give me than I'm acknowledging. If I get too specific, I may miss out on His Goodness altogether. By limiting the expected miracle to my specifications, I may not recognize His actual provision and answer to my prayer.

Instead, we have to pray expecting the full pendulum swing, from God's extravagant unlimited provision, all the way over to His training us and sparing us by holding back what would become burdensome or overwhelming to us. We have got to yield somehow to full-spectrum possibilities and still be grateful that whatever that means, we can expect His best for us.

It's true, praying Scripture and declaring back to God His promises to us, is powerful and even pleasing to Him because He knows it builds our faith and readies our hearts for His answer. Telling Him how we feel and crying out our complaints to Him is cathartic for us and more than acceptable to Him. He loves our honesty. Presenting Him our boo-boos to kiss and make better causes our Daddy to tenderly kneel down for us. So, when does "declaring" cross over the line to "demanding"? I think it's when we know we have it all figured out. We can see just how it should be, and if only God would listen to us and do His part like He promised then everything would be fine and dandy. If only God would! Driven, we find Scripture to prove our point and try to coerce God into keeping up His end of the deal.

Declaring God's Word back to Him in prayer is not for His sake, to remind Him or convince Him. It's for OUR sake, to humble us and remind US of His sovereignty and faithfulness. "Humble yourselves before the Lord and He will lift you up" (James 4:10). We need to come to Him like a little one with reaching arms asking, "Up, please?"

trusting in His being our Daddy, in the strength of His arms that would never drop us, and in the love of His heart that will patiently listen to ours.

It's kinda like the humility it takes to allow Jesus into our messy lives to help clean up the overwhelming clutter. It comes from trusting that His love and acceptance of us is not affected by our weak spots and failures. Trust gives us the freedom to open our door and confidently invite Him in. That's how we receive the answers and healing He has for us. The fear of Him scolding us is pushed out by His perfect love for us. There is nothing to hide and no one to impress. Think of how believing that would change your conversations with Him. Let me show you what I mean.

Is there a friend or relative in your life right now that you can completely be yourself with — one you don't censor your words for? You can just tell them what you're thinking and know they'll understand, smoothing out the rough edges and tossing out what doesn't make sense. Can you ride in the car together or go out to eat with them and not have to make conversation? You can just sit together on a porch swing in comfortable silence and watch the world go by? If so, you are very blessed.

That is the kind of relationship God is hoping to have with us, and He desires that our prayers would reflect that. But somehow between the Garden of Eden and now, walking and talking in the cool of the evening with Creator God has become talking TO God a few minutes before bedtime or crying out to Him from a foxhole. And we call it "saying our prayers."

Okay, so let's imagine that your trusted friend on the porch swing is named Joe. And you decide to go for a walk with him and insist on having a meaningful conversation because you just read an article that said it was important to talk. Just imagine if this is what your "conversation" sounded like:

[Take a deep breath and read through quickly without pausing. See if it reminds you of anything.]

My Good Friend, Joe, have you seen the news about that fire in the next town? Joe, there's so much bad stuff going on, Joseph. Maybe you should do something for that poor family. You could sell your car or something, Joe, and give them the money. Nobody would buy my car or I'd do it. So maybe, Good Friend, you could do something instead, Joseph. You have some extra bucks anyhow I'm sure. You're going to Florida again this winter right, Joe? Yeah, see? You got extra. I deserve to get away too ya know, Joseph. Maybe you could fly me down to visit with you, Joe. I do enough for you, Joseph, don't I? I mean, I try to be a good friend. I'm a good friend to you, right? I try to keep you happy and not offend you, Joe, and that's not easy 'cause you're so easily offended. I'm sorry if I offended you, but Joe, please forgive me and take me to Florida this year, okay? Good Friend? I think talking like this is the right thing to do, Joseph, don't you? Really, we should do this like every day. OK, Joe. We'll do it again... real soon. Amen?

Remind you of anything? How might your "conversation" with God differ if you understood Him to be a trusted Friend? You probably wouldn't have to remind Him, or yourself, of His Name so much. And maybe there would be moments of pausing to hear what He had to say? Maybe there would be natural stretches of just walking without any talking.

Sometimes prayer isn't about talking at all. A dear wise mother of some good friends of ours, who was also a high school English teacher, used to tell her students, "Do the task at hand with love." That spoke to me on so many levels, and influenced what became my life's key phrase: "Check your motivation. If it's not love, don't bother." But at the core was Mrs. Northridge's words of wisdom. And as I thought about prayer, I realized God IS love and to do anything WITH God is actually doing the task at hand with Love Himself. Having such an awareness of God's presence is like sitting on the porch swing with Him, not talking, just watching the world go by. Your life WITH Him becomes a prayer.

But there ARE times when prayer IS all about talking, like saying grace before a meal as our character, Roger, is about to find out:

"A Little Child Shall Lead Them"

SCENE: A banquet hall set with tables and chairs. It's just before the beginning of an Awards Banquet. People are milling around. Roger is standing off to one side, closest to audience, when Sam approaches him.

[LIGHTS UP]

SAM: Hey Roger, Roger you go to church, right?

ROGER: Yeah, why?

SAM: Look Rog, the clergyman guy can't make it here in time for the start of the banquet.

ROGER: Yeah, so?

SAM: So we need you to say the blessing before we eat.

ROGER: Why?

SAM: Because this whole "Outstanding Young Citizen Award" thing was the Clergy Association's idea so we have to say grace.

ROGER: No, I mean why me? I can't pray.

SAM: Aw, come on Roger, you said you go to church. You must know how to pray.

ROGER: Well I know how, it's just that I don't usually pray in front of 150 people.

SAM: But you know how to, right?

ROGER: Well yeah, I guess I do.

SAM: Great! You've got five minutes to come up with a humdinger of a blessing. You have to set a good example for all those children out there receiving awards. And don't forget to mention them. Oh, and the local cable company is broadcasting it live. So make it good.

ROGER: But I…

SAM [Exiting]: Thanks, Roger… I owe you.

ROGER: You're gonna owe me big time, buddy. Pray!
[RECORDING]: (As if the audience is hearing his thoughts) How do I pray? It used to be easy when I was a kid. Every night: Now I lay me down to sleep I pray the Lord my soul to keep. Wait… what was that grace one? God is great, God is good, let us thank Him for our food? I can't say that. They'll think they're in preschool. I know. I'll use Thee's and Thou's. That sounds like I know what I'm doing, and I heard somewhere God hears you better when you use Bible language. Almighty Creator, Thou hast broughtst us hither to this banquet for Thou artst great, Thou artst good, we thank Thee now for our foodst. Nah, they'll recognize it. How can I do this without sounding like an idiot? Latin! That'll do it. That will sound real impressive. But I don't know any Latin… They're gonna be expecting something poetic and inspiring and all I can give them is Mother Goose with a Shakespearian twist… We thank Thee now for our foodst. Forget it. I can't do this. I'll just have to tell Sam. [Sam and Jeremy enter.] (Out loud) I can't do this. I don't know how to pray.

SAM: That's okay, Roger. This young man overheard me talking and he volunteered.

ROGER: He's gonna say grace?

SAM: Yup!

ROGER: Oh, the God is great, God is good one?

JEREMY: No.

ROGER: You know another one?

JEREMY: Kind of.

ROGER: Well you can't say "Now I lay me down to sleep."

JEREMY: I know that.

ROGER: What are you gonna say then?

JEREMY: I'm gonna tell God thank you.

ROGER: How?

JEREMY: I'm gonna talk to Him.

ROGER: But how?

JEREMY: Just like I'm talking to you.

ROGER: You can do that?

JEREMY: Sure.

ROGER: And He still hears you?

JEREMY: Yeah!

ROGER: But what about all the people out there. They're gonna be listening too, ya know.

JEREMY: I'm not talking to them. I'm talking to God and God already knows what I'm gonna say.

SAM: Hey guys, we better get going. The natives are getting restless. (To Roger) You coming?

ROGER: Better believe it, I gotta hear this. Imagine that. Praying is just talking to God. Who'da thought?

[BLACKOUT]

Giving honor, paying tribute, saying thank You, are all about responding to God. Making requests and confessions, petitions and apologies, are all about talking to Him. What we want to avoid is talking AT Him. Nobody likes to be talked at. Even our posture can't make up for it. Bowing your head with pious, pleading hands, or even kissing someone's feet, can't make up for a heart standing arrogantly on the inside demanding, "My will be done, not Yours!"

Kevin MacDonald, the same prophetic evangelist that prophesied, "It's time to get back on the horse," spoke one evening about "prayer" and though I'm not a note-taker, I wrote this one down:

> When you pray, pray with open hands, not literally open hands, though there's nothing wrong with that, but hands open and ready to receive WHATEVER God has for you. In the verse, Ask and it shall be given, "Ask" equals "request with an open heart."

Being specific when you request things is being honest about what you desire, but what if God has something so much better for you, or for the person for whom you're praying? Would you want Him to stick to YOUR plan, you, with your hands folded so nicely and your eyes closed not peeking? For sure, it's good to be honest when you pray, and even being specific can be okay as long as you give Him permission to be God and do what's best. We can be sure His best for us will be done if we humbly pray Scripture [Okay, so here comes Peter Cottontail, I know, but I think the bunny trail is worth the trip] or if we pray in tongues.

Praying in tongues or declaring the Words of God are the most powerful weapons of warfare there are! The devil and his minions have no defense against them. The Word of God is our two-edged sword (Hebrews 4:12) separating bone from marrow, exposing the very infrastructure of a dilemma or demonic assignment. I heard it preached once that the list of spiritual armor God instructs us to wear (Ephesians 6:13-18) is not supposed to end with "the Sword of the Spirit which is the Word of God." Instead, the next sentence, which begins, "And pray…" should actually be translated from the original Greek to, "by praying." So, the direction given (starting in verse 17) should read: "Take up the helmet of salvation and the Sword of the Spirit, which is the Word of God, BY PRAYING in the Spirit on all occasions…"

Speaking in tongues (except at Pentecost) was not often spoken of in the Baptist Church where I was raised and where I served most of my life. I asked Jesus into my heart to be my Savior when I was seven years old and I was baptized in water when I was nine. I can remember when I was alone as a kid, and just for fun, speaking in gibberish, like making up a foreign language. I thought every kid did that. I always felt so happy just chattering away and not thinking or caring about having any of it make sense or sound intelligent. It was just for fun. As I grew up and compared notes with my adult friends, I found out they did not share my make-up-your-own-language-for-fun playtime experience. I felt rather silly, but consoled myself with, "Must be a sign of creativity."

When my husband and I started operating in the gifts of healing and deliverance, a friend explained to me that speaking in tongues can be a tool in our spiritual tool belt and a powerful weapon of warfare especially in healing and deliverance. I lived most of my life filled with the Spirit, inspired, protected, assisted, and guided by Him without ever using a prayer language. My husband, Steve, had been given the gifts of healing, seeing miracles and sensing words of knowledge, without ever speaking in tongues. But I trusted my friend. She was a pastor and wise counselor and I knew she wouldn't steer me wrong. "Hey, if God wants me to have another tool, I want it!" I was reminded of my gibberish kid language and when I told her about it she smiled, "Gibberish, huh?" We prayed together that evening with some other friends who also wanted a prayer language and when we were done she asked, "Still think it was gibberish?" I'm so grateful for her sensitivity and encouragement and that God put someone in my path who could share a Biblical perspective about praying in tongues without all the drama and dogma. It was even more confirmation that this gift was a blessing and a weapon God wanted me to have.

I'm not trying to argue or prove anything here. I just want to share our experience and encourage you to be fearless and trust God to give you ALL that He has for you to complete your mission. As we practiced and used our prayer language in ministry, Steve and I felt catapulted to a new level of warfare and effectiveness. The fear of it or forbidding of it could only be caused by the father of lies. Seems to me the devil's minions are on a mission to eradicate speaking in tongues because it scares them powerless.

I don't know if you've noticed that the amperage of warfare has greatly increased and the dark arts have subtly infiltrated into all aspects of our culture. We have been strategically placed where we are at this moment to take back territory and conquer evil. It's a supernatural war we are fighting and it's fought in two different realms — physical and spiritual. We are spiritual beings in physical bodies, so we get to fight in both realms at the same time.

God has called us into this war as soldiers of prayer, as mouthpieces trumpeting Truth, wielding Swords of the Spirit. If we heard and understood everything our Commander was doing, we'd collapse under the intensity of it. The beauty and uniqueness of a prayer language (praying in tongues) is to be able to declare God's orders and commands by submitting to the power of the Holy Spirit without understanding at times what we're actually declaring into the spiritual realm. God is using us, but protecting us from knowing things that could alarm us. It's like being a secret agent with a coded message that must be delivered to someone in charge, but you have no idea what it means. "The purple dog barks twice at the low flying orange sparrow," could be the confirmation signal to a division of heavenly armies to take down a stronghold over your town and YOU are the chosen one to deliver it. We don't understand it, but we know it's important and we follow through with our mission — praying in the Spirit on all occasions. Pray without ceasing.

There are other times though, that we need to know exactly what the Holy Spirit is prompting us to pray so that our faith, and the faith of those around us, will increase. When praying Scripture or praying in tongues, we know that whatever we request will be done because we know it's in accordance with God's Will. We're praying His very Words! The Holy Spirit will give us the interpretation of our prayers (as well as words of knowledge) and remind us of God's promises in Scripture, especially when we're praying for physical healing for someone else. They need to know that God knows exactly what needs healing and that it's God's Will for them to be healed. God knows we ALL need our faith to be built up like that.

From God's Word we know that the Cross and the whipping post, the Blood and stripes of Jesus, make the redemption of our bodies, souls, and spirits possible. They prove God's Will for us. That's why we can pray for healing every time knowing it's God's Will, as much as knowing salvation is always God's Will. But just like salvation (healing and life to our spirits) is a choice and requires God's grace, our faith and acceptance, so also healing of our bodies and souls is a choice and requires the same.

Our faith increases when we read in God's Word that it is His Will that none should perish and everyone who calls on the Name of the Lord will be saved (2 Peter 3:9, Acts 2:21). But do people still perish? Is everyone saved? Does that prove it's not always God's Will? Of course not. Then why is it any harder to believe that it's always God's Will for us to be healed? Just because you prayed for healing and didn't see it, doesn't negate that God's Word is true. Matthew 8:16–17 says Jesus drove out spirits with a word and healed ALL the sick to fulfill Isaiah 53:4, "He took up our infirmities and carried our diseases." He told many their sins were forgiven because He knew the Cross was coming. He healed the sick the same way, knowing He'd pay for it later. It's what Jesus took the beating and torture for on the whipping post. He was already going to be crucified. Why the brutal flogging? Why the stripes and crown of thorns? By His wounds and stripes we are physically healed, by His death on the cross we are forgiven and saved from the curse, and by His resurrection we are justified. That is God's Will! Is everyone saved? Is everyone healed? Is everyone justified? It's still His Will that they would be. Isn't it?

Who do you think started the rumor that physical healing and miracles are a thing of the past and were only to prove the first apostles were authentic representatives of the Gospel (or that praying in tongues is spooky and possibly evil)?

When Jesus preached His Good News to the multitudes, what did He preach? What did He instruct His teams of two to preach, those

He sent out to surrounding towns to cast out demons and heal the sick? What was the gospel message that they spread? He hadn't been crucified or resurrected yet. The Jews weren't looking for how to get to heaven. They knew the truth from Scripture that Paradise was going to be restored to earth. They were looking for the Kingdom of God to come to them. They were looking for a Messiah King to bring their nation restoration and freedom from oppression and political bondage. So that's what Jesus preached — the Good News that the Kingdom of God is at hand, standing in front of you:

> I'm here. But it's not what you think. It's so much more than you expect or what you've been praying for. Surprise! It's healing of your bodies, freedom from demonic oppression, and forgiveness of every sin you'll ever commit. Look, I'll prove it! Do you trust Me? I have healing and deliverance for you. Do you want it? I have freedom from the burdens of man-made laws that only blind you to My grace. I bring to you restoration of sight and hope. Can you see it? Listen. Do you recognize My voice? I sound just like My Dad. Can you hear Me? I'm the Good Shepherd. My sheep know My voice. Now do what I do, and when I leave and send you power from on High, demonstrate My love and do even greater things than these.

Does that mean we're supposed to be super teachers and preachers? Is that all Jesus did? Teach and preach?

If our enemy has an arsenal of supernatural tricks and counterfeit spiritual gifts, shouldn't our authentic gifts of the Holy Spirit be incredibly powerful and supernatural, signs and wonders, miracles and healing, restorative to spirit, soul and body? Why would God allow the enemy a bazooka and give His own kids a pop-gun? How could He say, "Greater is He that is in you than he that is in the world"[2] and not prove it today with miracles, signs, and wonders? That's the power of prayer — the manifestation of faith that God's promises bring restoration and freedom! Now that is Good News! Not some future promise that only comes true when we die.

---

[2] 1 John 4:4

Our prayers are power-fed by the Holy Spirit who raised Jesus from the dead, giving Him His eternal body clothed in Glory, even more glorious than the first Adam. Jesus IS the King of Glory, Mighty to save, Majestic and True! Hallelujah! That same Spirit who raised Jesus, lives IN us and declares life and truth through our prayers and proclamations. He brings health to our bodies and nourishes our souls each time we declare His Word and share His Love. Each time we pray for others, we receive back a blessing. "With the measure you use it will be measured to you... Give and it will be given pressed down and running over" (Luke 6:33).

Jesus taught us to present our requests to the Father humbly, reverently, and simply. No need to beg or plead our case. And certainly, we have no right to demand anything. We should save all our demanding for when we take authority over demonic forces (including afflicting spirits of illness or torment).

I remember the day when I was being frightened by a demonic encounter and I prayed to God to deliver me from the evil one by crying out, "God, please make it go away!" He had helped me so many times before, but this time He said, "No, Honey, you do it." It was like when my dad took the training wheels off my bike but held the back of my seat and ran alongside me. I wobbled but I didn't fall down. I said to the demon, "No. I'm not afraid of you. His kingdom rules over ALL. Go away!" It left. And my Daddy God let go of my bike and applauded me. No person had told me how to do that. But just that morning I had read Psalm 103:19, "The Lord has established His throne in Heaven, and His Kingdom rules over all." It impressed me enough to try to memorize it. God gave me my Sword before sending me into battle. He trained my hands for war. I submitted to God, resisted the devil, and it fled. I felt so empowered. It was the beginning of overcoming so many fears.

So see, my bunny trail led us right back to prayer and even set up the next chapter on overcoming fear. But let's declare and stand together with this Sword in our hands. Read this out loud with me: [Go ahead. You can even stand up. Okay, well, at least stand up on the inside.]

Devote yourselves to prayer, being watchful and thankful…
Be joyful always, pray continually, give thanks in all circumstances.
Rejoice in the Lord always… The Lord is near.
Do not be anxious about anything, but in everything by prayer
and petition, with thanksgiving, present your requests to God.
And the peace of God, which transcends all understanding will guard
your hearts and minds in Christ Jesus"

(from Colossians 4:2, 1st Thessalonians 5:17-18, Philippians 4:4-7).

The power and importance of prayer cannot be emphasized enough. It's vital not only for victory, but for survival in these last days of human government before Jesus returns to earth to reign. I'd like to start a revolution if you'll help me. If you ever hear yourself, or anyone else say, "All we can do is pray," replace it immediately with, "All we NEED to do is pray!" Everything else is like boiling some water when a mother is in labor. It's only helpful because it gives the dad something to do to keep him busy.

The real labor... is prayer!

Chapter 7: Can't Be Too Careful... or Can You?

/FEAR

SCENE: The living room of a small apartment. Ursula, an eccentric older woman, is mesmerized in fear. She is watching TV and is about to be joined by her equally eccentric older sister.

[LIGHTS UP. Knock at the door.]

URSULA (Suspiciously): Who is it?

MATILDA [Offstage]: It's me!

URSULA: Who's me?

MATILDA: Who's me?! Your sister, who else?

URSULA: What's your name?

MATILDA: You losing your memory already? You can't remember your own sister's name?

URSULA: Oh I know my sister's name. But how do I know you're really my sister? What's your name?

MATILDA: Ursula, let me in. I just walked three blocks from the bus stop after riding a half hour next to a very talkative four-year-old who was obsessed with Barney and wouldn't stop singing (Sings loudly and off key) "I love you, you love me we're a happy family..."

URSULA [Unlocking many locks]: Alright! Alright, Matilda, it's you! I'm convinced. Nobody else could sing like that.

MATILDA [Enters with arms opened.]: Ursulaaaa!

URSULA: Matildaaaa! [They hug.]

MATILDA [Cuffs her head]: Why didn't you let me in sooner. My feet are killing me. [Sits down]

URSULA: Can't be too careful, you know. There are plenty of crazy people out there that would love to get their hands on a prize such as moi.

MATILDA: Yeah, they'd have to be crazy alright.

URSULA: Excuse me?

MATILDA: Can't be too careful you're right.

URSULA [Sits down]: You're here. After all this time, you finally came to visit. I can't believe it. What took you so long?

MATILDA: Hey, you're the one with the car. How come you didn't just pop over to see me?

URSULA: I can't use my car anymore.

MATILDA: Oh... did it breakdown?

URSULA: No, but it could. That's why I don't drive. I could be out there somewhere and have the darn thing croak in the middle of the highway or something. Then what would I do?

MATILDA: Call a tow truck.

URSULA (Ignoring her): I could get a flat tire, or the whole wheel could fall off, or another car could cut me off and send me into a tailspin, or it might start to rain and the windows would get all fogged up and I'd have to slam on the brakes and the guy behind me would be too slow and he'd plow into me and the car behind him would plow into the both of us. Before you know it, we'd all be stuck. Then what would I do?

MATILDA: Call a tow truck… or an ambulance.

URSULA: An ambulance?! You see what I mean? You could get killed out there! That's why I don't drive.

MATILDA: Hot diggety! I can have your car then, right?

URSULA: Oh no, Matilda. I couldn't let you risk your life like that.

MATILDA: You'd rather I'd be tortured by a four-year-old singing (Starts singing loudly) "I love you, you love…"

URSULA (Interrupts): Alright! Alright! I'll get you the keys. [Exits to kitchen]

MATILDA: While you're out there, I could use some lunch. I'm starving. Whatcha got? Any pizza?

URSULA [From offstage]: No, too much cholesterol.

MATILDA: Soup?

URSULA: Too much sodium.

MATILDA: Salad?

URSULA: Pesticides and preservatives.

MATILDA: Bread?

URSULA: Bromate flour.

MATILDA: A cup of coffee?

URSULA: [Enters with keys] Caffeine can kill you, ya know.

MATILDA: What DO you have?

URSULA: Tofu and twice-filtered pure spring water.

MATILDA: My feet are feeling much better. Let's go out to lunch, okay? [Gets up and heads to the door]

URSULA: We can't do that.

MATILDA: [Turns] For Pete's sake, why not?

URSULA: You have no idea of what they put into the food out there, do you?

MATILDA: I've heard they use things that are edible. Not some synthetically produced soy muck that has no taste. Tofu? How can you even look at the stuff?

URSULA: I'm just being careful what I eat. Have you ever even tried tofu? I'll go get you some.

MATILDA: I'm not hungry.

URSULA: But you just said you were starving.

MATILDA: I meant thirsty. Maybe just some water.

URSALA: But tofu is good for you, Matilda. It's the one food that hasn't been reported to have any adverse side effects in laboratory animals.

MATILDA: That's because they can't get the rats to eat it. Come on, Ursula. Let's go to Burgerama and live a little.

URSULA: I'm not eating that stuff.

MATILDA: Then just come with me.

URSULA: But Matilda, we could get mugged or something.

MATILDA: In broad daylight?

URSULA: Doesn't matter. I watch the news. There are thugs and robbers everywhere. Two delicate, attractive beauties such as ourselves are prime targets for those nasty criminals.

MATILDA (Getting caught up): You could be right.

URSULA: It's awful. Everywhere you turn, murders and stabbings.

MATILDA (Eyes widening): Burglaries and muggings.

URSULA: Death and destruction are practically knocking at the door.

[Knock at the door. They both jump.]

URSULA: Oh, Matilda!

MATILDA: Oh, Ursula!

[They clutch one another.]

URSULA: What do we do?

MATILDA: Call 911.

URSULA: Right, 911. [Still clinging to each other, they scurry in sync to the phone.] What's the number?

MATILDA: 9… uh… 1-1.

URSULA: What should I say?

MATILDA: What should you say?

URSULA: What should I say?

MATILDA: Tell 'em there's someone at the door.

URSULA: Right. Hello? There's someone knocking at my door. What should I do?

[Knock at the door]

MATILDA: Wait a minute! Wait a dog gone minute! [Hangs up the phone]

URSULA: Matilda, what are you doing?! Someone is knocking at my door. They were gonna tell me what to do.

MATILDA: I know what to do.

URSULA: What?

MATILDA: Answer the door.

URSULA: It's death I tell you, certain death!

[Another knock on the door]

URSULA: Death is knocking at my door and you're gonna ask it right in. [She screams as Matilda starts to open door.]

MATILDA: [Opens door and gets newspaper] Death delivers the Boston Herald now.

URSULA: Oh no! (Catching breath) That was close.

MATILDA: Yeah, close alright. You almost had me as scared as you.

URSULA: It could have been an axe murderer.

MATILDA: All this fear has made me hungry.

URSULA: I couldn't eat if you paid me.

MATILDA: Well, I'll call Pizza Palace and have them deliver me a one-person, large-sized, smothered in anchovies pizza, extra cheese.

URSULA: But the delivery person may not be on the up and up. They may check out the apartment and spread the word that 203 Pleasant Drive, Apt. 3C is the place to hit. I watch Crime Busters on TV. I know how the criminal mind works.

MATILDA (Playing into it): You shouldn't watch TV you know. I heard it emits too much radiation.

URSULA: You did? It does?

MATILDA: Sure, everybody knows that. Don't sit too close to the screen or you'll start glowing. I'm gonna go out and get some lunch and some fresh air. I'll be back in a little while. Lock the door. Don't answer the phone, could be a prank call. And don't stand by the window.

URSULA: Why not?

MATILDA: Drive by shootings. (Teasing her) You never know. [Exits]

URSULA: [Paces anxiously, then opens hallway door and yells] Matilda, if someone attacks you, just SING!

[BLACKOUT]

Next to laughing, yawning, and all the coughing that suddenly happens in an audience during a moment of silence, I think one of the most contagious things we experience in life is fear. One little chicken thinks the sky is falling, and suddenly the whole town is in a frenzy. But unlike laughter, which is proven to promote healing, fear can paralyze us or make us weak in the knees, and at times actually cause us to become physically sick. It makes me wonder if there really is such a thing as "healthy" fear.

We are born with God-given survival instincts, fear of danger being one of them. God wants us to have an awareness of harmful objects or situations so we can avoid them or take action when our lives are threatened. As long as the fear object is both present and powerful, flight or fight is a healthy response. If either or both components of danger are missing, fear becomes unhelpful and potentially unhealthy.

This example helped me understand the difference: If a rattlesnake was rattling away next to your feet and adrenaline caused you to jump away in fear, that's healthy. The snake was both present and potent. If a dead rattlesnake lying there stiff as a stick did the same thing to you, that would be unnecessary fear. It was present but not at all powerful. If just the thought of the rattlesnake, as you're reading this, makes your adrenaline pump, that's a controlling kind of fear causing you unfounded distress. It's unhealthy fears that limit us and keep us from experiencing our Blood-bought freedom in Christ.

Unfounded fears are always based on a lie. We're either giving the object more power/potency than it has, or we're thinking it's actually present when it's only present in our imagination. That includes all the "what if" thoughts we have: What if the elevator cable snaps? What if the bridge collapses? What if he stops loving me? What if we crash?

Notice all the question marks? They are an indication of uncertainty. "Now faith is being sure of what we hope for and certain of what we do not see" (Hebrews 11:1). But when we're sure that doom awaits us and we're certain that our future is bleak because that's how we see it — our faith has become fear. When uncertainty of God's promises creeps in, we become sure and certain of things we dread. Most of what we dread boils down to three basic fears — fear of man, fear of death, and fear of satan. Underneath those three, looms the undercurrent of physical or emotional pain. And even though we understand pain to be a healthy indicator of which actions to avoid or what part of us needs special attention, we tend to do whatever it takes to keep ourselves pain free.

Fear of man generates fears of financial loss, embarrassment, failure, public speaking, homelessness, rejection, marriage, divorce, confrontation, disapproval, punishment, and even fear of being victimized or falsely accused. It can be used by the enemy to keep us from fulfilling our destiny. Think of how many times you didn't do or say something because you were afraid of what people might think. God has been trying for years to work this fear out of me. It has kept me from public speaking, praying for people in the marketplace, and up to this point, publishing a book. It's time to fear GOD only, not man.

Fear of death can appear to be healthy. We are wired for survival, programmed to avoid death. But since most of us haven't experienced it and can only imagine what death is like, the mysterious unknown can easily turn our survival instincts into fear.

If you have an imagination like me, then you can bring any scenario straight to death. Hangnail? = Infection, blood poisoning, kidney failure... death. Bridge over water? = Seagull hits the windshield, veer off course, avoid oncoming truck, over guardrail, underwater, trapped in seatbelt... death. Carnival? = Avoid fried foods, have cotton candy instead, inhale sugar, sweetness chokes me, throat closes… death. I bet you thought I was going to talk about the unsafe, loosely bolted, assembled-too-hastily carnival rides, but that would have been too amateur.

Can you see how if your major fear is death, there are a lot of minor fears based on it? God never intended us to fear death. He doesn't want us to be afraid of anything. That's why Jesus took the sting out of death for us by experiencing, in our place, the most horrible kind of death ever invented, absorbing all the effects of death-causing sin into His sinless body and burying them forever in hell on our behalf. With His new, resurrected, immortal body came the promise that those who trust in His Life-giving Blood will never experience the trauma of death but will simply fall asleep and wake up in Heaven's realm, no fear necessary. The sting of death is gone, and we are promised our own immortal bodies when Jesus returns to the earth.

Fear of satan comes when we are deceived into believing that spiritual enemies of the Lord Jesus Christ have power and authority over us. One of the perks, a very BIG perk, of trusting and following Jesus is that He gives US the authority and power. We have been given the authority to trample on snakes and scorpions, to overcome all the power of the enemy so that nothing can harm us (Luke 10:19). Psalm 91 tells us that we will tread upon the lion and the cobra, we will trample the great lion and the serpent, and God has commanded His angels concerning us to guard us in all our ways.

Fearing satan is saying he is more powerful than God. That's basically backwards worship. Giving satan that kind of credit can open us up to mental and emotional torment, fears of darkness, of never being loved, of going crazy, of being inadequate or vulnerable. And as crazy as it sounds, we can develop a fear of truth. Since truth counteracts the grip of the enemy's lies, if we're living oppressed and tormented by demonic influence, truth being spoken can provoke demons to cause uneasy feelings, physical pain, and an increase of mental harassments. It becomes more comfortable for us to avoid listening to the truth, so we tend to stay away from people and places where truth is celebrated.

As fearful of just about everything as I was, fearing satan, I think, was the biggest source of torment for me. That is why my heart's desire is to see people delivered and set free by knowing the truth of their authority in Christ Jesus and experiencing the power of His Holy Spirit working in and through them.

All the voices I heard in my head, like a committee bouncing ideas and opinions around, I thought was just part of being creative. Lots of creative people I know have their own committees. But now that my committee has been disarmed and disbanded, I realize how much imagination plays a part in creativity and how much the devil can take advantage of it to cause unfounded fear.

There are all kinds of reasons we can end up with overactive imaginations. When painful or scary circumstances force us into imagining life differently in order to cope, we can get really good at imagining. But the downside is we can get really good at imagining, and instead of seeing things as they really are or better, the fear and pain catch up and we imagine the worst. It takes much practice, lots of faith, and believing in the truth of God's presence and power to retrain our imaginations to be used for good. Imagination, by itself, can only get you so far:

"Where's Your Happy Place?"

SCENE: Starts in a lobby of an apartment building on Christmas Eve. Mother and daughter are waiting for the elevator.

[LIGHTS UP]

DEANNA: Aw come on, Mom. I'm tired.

DEE: So you think it's my fault the elevator's taking this long.

DEANNA: Isn't everything your fault?

DEE: You are so 14.

DEANNA: Where is it?

DEE: They used to have...

DEANNA: When you were a kid?

DEE: Yeah, there was an indicator on the outside of the elevator above the doors...

DEANNA: Did they even have elevators back then?

DEE: Very funny! Anyway, you could tell by the indicator which floor the elevator was stopped on.

DEANNA: So?

DEE: So, then you'd know where it was and you wouldn't have to annoy your mother with such questions.

DEANNA: How about not annoying your daughter with irrelevant stories.

DEE: It was relevant.

[Cheryl enters and stands off to the side to wait for the elevator.]

DEANNA (Confidentially to Dee): Who's that?

DEE [Shrugs, then to Cheryl]: Hello.

CHERYL (Nervously. Looking at floor): Hello.

DEE: Elevator's really slow tonight.

CHERYL: Slow? Do you think there's a problem? I hate elevators. Are there stairs?

DEANNA: Yeah, right over there.

DEE: What floor are you going to?

CHERYL: The tenth.

DEE: Us too. That's a lot of flights to climb.

CHERYL: You don't understand. I am so phobic. I'm working on it, but I'm only up to six floors now.

DEE: Good for you.

CHERYL: I was only going to attempt ten cause that's where my nephew and his wife live. They're my only family and it's Christmas Eve. I thought I'd be brave.

DEANNA: What are their names?

CHERYL: His name is Jeffrey and...

DEANNA: Jeff and Karen?

CHERYL: Yeah, that's them.

DEANNA: They live across the hall from us.

DEE: They're so nice... Hey, we've lived here six years now and there's never been a problem with the elevator.

DEANNA: And we'll be with you the whole way.

CHERYL: I guess ten flights in heels is probably not the best idea. And there's never been a problem?

DEE: Not in six years. I just think there's lots of people getting on and off tonight, being Christmas Eve and all.

BRAD: [Enters with bottles clanking in a bag] Hey, Merry Christmas!

DEE: Merry Christmas. Last minute shopping?

BRAD: Yeah um, grocery shopping... um... stuff for dinner tomorrow.

DEANNA: How's Bailey?

BRAD: He's good. I got him a Christmas doggie treat for the morning, but he sniffed it out this afternoon, wrapping paper and all, all over the place.

[Imaginary elevator door opens.]

BRAD: Oh, that was quick.

[Brad gets in and turns around. Deanna gets on. Dee holds doors and talks to Cheryl.]

DEE: Whaddya think?

CHERYL: You sure there's never been a problem?

DEE: Not that I know of.

DEANNA: You could always ride up to the 6th floor and walk from there.

CHERYL (Deep breath): Okay. [Steps in]

[**FADE TO BLACK.** Then **LIGHTS COME UP** on Dee who's frozen like a deer in headlights, Brad near doors with his back to the audience, Deanna sitting on the floor at the back of the elevator listening to music with earphones, and Cheryl fanning Dee.]

DEE: How long has it been?

DEANNA: Seven minutes.

DEE: Is that all?

DEANNA: At least the screaming has stopped.

BRAD: [Turns around] Sorry 'bout that. I've never been stuck in an elevator before. Maybe we should break into my… um… my "groceries."

DEE: I don't think that's necessary. Besides, we have a minor among us. How long did they say it would be?

CHERYL: They're working on it. Maybe a couple more minutes.

BRAD: Like, is the elevator getting smaller?

CHERYL: Okay. Step one. My therapist says to remember to take slow deep breaths… nice and slowly in and out… in… and out. [They breathe.]

BRAD: Wait, I think I breathed out instead of in, is that okay?

DEE: I don't think there's enough air in here for us to be doing this. Maybe we should take turns holding our breath.

BRAD: You first.

CHERYL: Wait a minute, now. The fan is still circulating the air. There's plenty of fresh air flooding this nice, roomy, well-ventilated...

BRAD: Death trap! I tell you it's a death trap.

DEE: I think the walls are closing in.

CHERYL: Okay! Okay! Step two. Let's think of calm, lovely, peaceful things.

DEANNA: Like our happy place?

CHERYL: Exactly. Whatever makes you the most happy.

DEANNA: Christmas.

CHERYL: What about Christmas?

DEANNA: Shopping for presents, no, wrapping them, no wait, opening lots and lots of presents. I guess presents make me most happy, yeah presents!

CHERYL: Good. Presents. (Then to Brad) What about you?

BRAD: My happy place? Anywhere but tiny elevators.

CHERYL: What makes you most happy? Where do you go?

BRAD: Uh... a good party. Good friends, good times, if you know what I mean. Hence the name "Happy Hour." (To Dee) Hey if you change your mind? [Holds up his bag]

DEE: No, thank you. Thanks anyhow.

DEANNA: I know where your happy place is, Mom.

DEE: Where?

DEANNA: Bermuda.

DEE: You got that right. Actually, any place warm and away from the office, but Bermuda is where we honeymooned. Oh, I better call your father and tell him to use the stairs.

DEANNA: Dad, up ten flights of stairs? He won't make it here till New Years.

[Dee turns her back to the audience to make the call.]

DEANNA (To Cheryl): So where's your happy place?

CHERYL: Well up to now it's been the ocean and gentle breezes and waves lapping against the beach. That thought is what got me into an elevator in the first place and up to the sixth floor. But now that what I feared the most has actually happened and I'm still alive, I think what really matters most is that the...

BRAD: Is that the doors are open!

DEE: The doors are open!

DEANNA: Oh good. What floor are we on?

DEE: The ninth.

BRAD: What do you know, my floor.

DEANNA: Should we try for one more?

EVERYONE ELSE: NO!

DEE: We'll walk thank you very much.

BRAD: Merry Christmas everybody! [Exiting opposite] We'll remember this one, huh?

[Everyone else ad lib, Oh yeah. Merry Christmas. Sure will. Etc.]

DEANNA (To Brad): Say hi to Bailey for me.

BRAD: I will.

DEANNA (As exiting): So, what were you saying? Before the doors opened?

CHERYL: About what?

DEANNA: Ya know, where's YOUR happy place now?

[BLACKOUT]

Facing our fears by imagining our happy place can only get us to about the sixth floor. To overcome fear for good, we have to trust in God's power and presence, and use the authority Jesus has given us to be more than conquerors.

Our imaginations, I believe, were given to us as a place to meet with God. It's a place where spirit and mind overlap. It's where visions, dreams, and creativity happen. Imagination is a realm God created in us where we, as humans, can see into another dimension and dare to believe the impossible — no limitations. So when you think, "Did I just imagine that?" chances are you did... but it wasn't just your imagination.

It would make perfect sense that the enemy would try as hard as he does to control our imaginations with fear and cloud our thinking with darkness, especially when we're children. Since fear, unforgiveness, and habitual sin are the three things that allow demons to invade our lives, and young children are very forgiving and not apt to have harmful addictions, fear is what's left. The devil has a field day by exploiting a young one's basic survival instincts, as he tries to gain access through scary dreams, shadowy figures, and monsters under the bed or in a dark closet.

Nobody had to tell us they were there. We just knew. To be told by a grown up that monsters aren't real and not to be afraid is only half right. We don't have to be afraid. God is so much bigger. Jesus is our Protector and Avenger. But demons are real and they don't play fair.

Children, as well as adults, need to know that Jesus is our Good Shepherd, and even if things are dark and scary, we don't have to be afraid because Jesus is right here with us and He carries a great big rod and a staff to keep us safe and beat up scary things.

If we only remember from childhood the part about "what we're afraid of isn't really real" and we're told to overcome it by using mind over matter, as we get older, we can easily find ourselves in some pretty dark valleys. Add to that the fact that grown-up unforgiveness and habitual sin open up even more doors to demonic taunts, and we can easily start to feel unworthy of the Good Shepherd's protection. Our dark valley becomes even darker with confliction, guilt and frustration.

"I Shall Not Want"

SCENE: A monologue performed center stage, lights out with a single spot that comes up dimly on the actor as he begins half-praying, half-talking to the audience.

PERSON: It's so dark. Why's it hafta be so dark? Where's the green pasture, huh? I thought if the Lord was my Shepherd it would mean, you know, green pastures and still waters? My life feels more like swampland. It stinks. It's too hard to keep going when every step is such an effort. So I try to go back to this and find some encouragement. The Lord is my Shepherd, I shall not want. Look, I don't want a mansion. I just want to be able to pay my mortgage on time… for once. And I'm not asking to go on a cruise. I just thought a weekend away would be nice. I need a break, too, you know. I'm tired. I'm tired of giving and pretending and telling myself that everything's gonna be okay. The Lord is my Shepherd, I will lack nothing… except energy, money, and time enough to get everything done. Too many people are demanding too much of me. I'm supposed to be able to be everything to everybody, go in 100 directions, and still walk in the same direction as the Shepherd. I'm ready to be restored now, if you hadn't noticed! A little oil would be nice too, you know... soothing, comforting oil, to take away this pain. Do you know what it's like to try and get up in the morning when you've been kept awake all night with pain? It's pretty hard to keep up when you can't even get up. Considering all, I think I do pretty well for myself... keeping up with Him. I may not always follow Him as closely as I could, I may not stay exactly on the paths of righteousness, but hey, sheep are supposed to wander, right? It gives the Shepherd something to do... chase the sheep. [Looks nervously around] But this time... this time I think I've wandered a bit too far. I didn't realize just how dark and cold it could get. I can't even see the Shepherd anymore. It's SO dark. Why does it hafta be so dark?

[FADES TO BLACK]

We think we've gone just too far off the path of righteousness, and the voice in our head says, "Don't call for help because:

a) No one can hear you."

b) Nobody really cares anyway."

c) You got yourself into this, you can get yourself out."

d) They'll think you're crazy and want to lock you up."

And besides "e) All of the above," I think an undertone most of us hear when we've wandered off track is, "You asked for this! Now live with it!"

When God has designed you to do some serious battle against the forces of darkness, the battle starts early on in life because the opposition is great. The enemy fears our potential and tries everything to keep us from reaching it. The intensity of warfare is felt even more when we seem backed into a corner and made to feel VERY alone. Like any successful animal kingdom predator knows, single out your prey, look for the weak or sick and then, if possible, isolate them even farther from their herd.

The moment we ask Jesus to be our Savior, it is written on our hearts to bear one another's burdens, confess to one another, pray for one another, stand together and walk in His grace with one another. We're urged to not judge or discriminate, condemn or ignore, but to love, above everything else, to love one another. Isolation is not an option, especially if you're wounded.

It's funny, I can remember as a kid, when the blanket over my head wasn't quite cutting it, and I'd finally find my voice to call for help (despite the demon threatening me if I made a sound), as soon as my mom or dad walked in the room, the demon had to leave. Now even if you're not convinced that demons exist and think it was all just my imagination, the fact that there's safety in numbers and that fear fled when someone stronger who loved me came into the room, proves my point.

If we can begin to understand that greater is the Holy Spirit in us than satan and all his minions combined, and that Jesus' covenant of love, sealed in His Blood, promises He'll never leave nor forsake us no matter what, we can begin to overcome that "all I have is a blanket over my head to protect me" mentality.

The perfect love of God casting out all fear of punishment erases the multiple-choice reasons we have NOT to call for help. It empowers us with authority to use the Name and Blood of Jesus, the written Word of God, and the spoken language of Holy Spirit (tongues) as weapons against fear and the powers of darkness.

We can overcome fear and help children understand their power and authority by using God's Word. James 4:7 gives us the steps to take:

Submit to God   [Say aloud: In Jesus' Name and because of His Blood]
Resist the devil   [I command any devils or scary things to go away.]
And he will flee   [And God says you have to go.]

Then quote 1 John 5:18 out loud, "Jesus keeps me safe and the evil one cannot harm me." Demons shudder at the Name of Jesus and hate to be reminded of His Blood. Because satan and his demons are created beings, like us, they cannot hear our thoughts. They speak into the spiritual realm and we hear it in our minds. But we have to speak back into the spiritual realm with our mouths to be heard by them. They can only know what you're thinking the same way people do, by your expressions, reactions, and what you say. They know what others have said to you. They know what they have said. They know what has affected you in the past and what pushes your buttons. Only God is all-knowing and everywhere-present, and only He can hear your thoughts. He knows every word before it reaches your tongue. But the enemy can only hear what you say aloud.

Singing praises to God or quoting Scripture is torturous to demons' ears. But fear, like a dog whistle, attracts them and screams, "This one is doubting God's power and presence! Time to pounce!" You might as well send out invitations and blow up some balloons. They'll bring the confetti and balloon-popping pins, one loud heart-jumping kaboom after another.

One of my favorite verses to fight with is 2 Timothy 1:7, which tells me I have not been given a spirit of fear but of power, love, and a sound mind (or discipline). What I just realized is that this verse plows over fear with a bulldozer of the Holy Spirit's attributes and knocks down the three main characteristics of fear:

1. Fear is evidence that you think something has more POWER than God.

2. Fear is the result of not believing that God LOVES you with His perfect love (which, according to 1 John 4:18, drives out fear).

3. Fear can play tricks with your MIND and make you feel unstable and unDISCIPLINED.

God's Holy Spirit is a Spirit of POWER, LOVE and a SOUND, DISCIPLINED MIND. He doesn't want us afraid. He wants us to trust in His character, trust in His promises, and trust that His power and presence far exceed the power and presence of anything else, anytime, anywhere. I heard Jesus say:

The battle belongs to Me, and I belong to you. I became YOUR Brother, part of your family, so you could say to anything that scares you, "I'm gonna tell my Big Brother on you!" You can call Me your Brother because we're related. We have the same Father now. I had to be able to fight in your shoes to win freedom from fear for you. Don't belittle My victory on your behalf, by fearing anything! Take heart! I have overcome the World. There is nothing left here I don't have under My feet. The curse has forever been reversed. The physical death of your body is the last effects of the curse. But death is soon to be no more. Your new, forever, redeemed body is My promise to you, and My Spirit of resurrection power in you is My deposit guaranteeing what's to come.

The closer you get to My heart, the less fear you will feel. Let go of everything the world has taught you. Listen only to My voice and what I have written to you. Be strong in ME and in the power of My might. You've got this because...

"I've Got You!"

Walking near the edge of the trail, I begin to fall.
My courage starts to fail. The path is spinning.
Suddenly I'm weak in the knees. I cannot see the forest
for the trees. My fear is winning. I turn around
to You behind me. You take the lead and then remind me:

"I've got you, it's too hard on your own. I've got you,
don't go it alone. I've got you, just hold onto My Hand.
When you can't understand, I've got you."

Hearing things go bump in the night and it's so dark,
I can't find the light. My heart is racing.

Pull the covers over my head and close my eyes shutting out
the dread of what I'm facing. Then I hear Your Voice remind me,
Night or day Your grace will find me.

And I've got You, it's too hard on my own. I've got You,
I'm never alone. I've got You, You'll not let go my hand.
Though I can't understand. I've got You!

Treading water deeper than me, a tide of doubt sweeps me out to sea. I'm going
under. Holding to whatever floats by, remembering when I was warm and dry,
I start to wonder. I thought this stuff was all behind me.
One more time will You remind me?

And I hear You say, "I've got you, it's too hard on your own.
I've got you, don't go it alone. I've got you, just hold onto
My Hand. When you can't understand, I've got you."

Chapter 8: Take a "Brake" /REST

SCENE: A mother and her four active children are in their kitchen getting ready to leave. Two of the boys are tossing a ball. The daughter is practicing dance moves, and the youngest is playing with small plastic blocks at the table. As the lights come up, the mother is frazzled looking at her calendar and her oldest son has stopped to answer the phone before going back to the chaos.

[Phone rings. **LIGHTS UP**]

STEPHEN: It's for you, Mom. [Hands Mom phone] It's Dr. Car, he said.

MOM: Hello?

DR.CAR: [From offstage speaking into a tinny sounding microphone] Mrs. Robinson, this is Gary from Doctor Car. I have some bad news concerning your station wagon. She's in rough shape.

MOM: She?

DR.CAR: Your car. I like to refer to them as "She." They're like women, you know? Treat 'em right and they run smooth and easy. Ignore 'em and you got real trouble.

MOM: Well, whatever. If there's a problem with the car you should talk to my husband. He's the one that has to pay for it. He'll be here in about 5 minutes if you wanna call back.

DR.CAR: Okey, dokey! Will do.

MOM: Bye. (To Jeremy) All right, your practice is at 4:30 right?

JEREMY: No, at 4.

STEPHEN: Mine's at 4:30.

MOM: Okay. (To Kim) And your dance class starts at…

KIM: 3:30.

MOM: Great. So we'll be 10 minutes late for dance class but 15 minutes early for basketball. I'll be able to make my dentist appointment just on time.

STEPHEN: What about me?

KIM: Can we leave now? I don't wanna miss warm-ups.

MOM: We have to wait for Daddy so we can take the van 'cause the car is getting fixed at Doctor Car's, and we don't want to walk, do we?

STEPHEN: How you gonna get me to practice?

KIM: The car is at the doctor's?

MOM: No. It's at the mechanics. That's just the name of the place. They call it Doctor Car because the mechanic is like a car doctor.

KIM: That's a stupid name.

MOM: I don't care what he calls himself as long as he fixes the car.

TIM: Can I have a snack?

MOM: You just had one.

TIM: Can I have another one?

MOM: No! Oh! Good! Dad's home. Come on you guys head out to the van.

STEPHEN: How are you gonna get me to practice if you're supposed to be at the dentist?

MOM: We'll figure it out on the way.

[DAD enters. Kids, except Tim, say "hi and bye" as they exit arguing over who sits in the front.]

MOM: Hi, Honey! Can I have your keys? I need to take the van. The station wagon's... (To the kids) It's Jeremy's turn to sit in front! No, you can sit in front on the way home. (To Dad) Listen, I gotta go... um... oh yeah, Doctor Car is supposed to be calling about some stuff that needs to be done. I wanted him to talk to you. I'll be back later. [Exits, then comes back] There's stuff for sandwiches in the refrigerator. Help yourself. [Exits]

DAD (To Tim): Did Mommy go to the doctor's today?

TIM: I dunno.

MOM: [Enters] Come on Timothy! You're supposed to go with Jeremy, right?

TIM: What about my Connect-a-blocks?

MOM: We'll pick them up later. Come on.

DAD: Did you see your doctor?

MOM: Last week. Why?

DAD: I didn't know you were sick.

TIM (Crying): But the cat could knock them on the floor and you said if you stepped on one more stupid little block, you'd throw them all away!

MOM: [Guiding Tim out the door] The cat's outside. Now please just get in the car, will ya? (To Dad) I'll talk to you later. I've just been tired. I gotta go. Kim's already late. [Exits]

DAD: Hope she's okay. [Looks in the refrigerator for supper]

[Phone rings]

DAD: Hello?

DR.CAR: Mr. Robinson?

DAD: Yeah.

DR.CAR: This is Doctor Car calling.

DAD: Yeah, hi!

DR.CAR: Your wife told me to call you back.

DAD: Right, she told me you were gonna be calling. Is there something wrong?

DR.CAR: Well, we gave her a good lookin' over and I hate to tell you this, but she's in pretty rough shape.

DAD: Really? Well, can you fix whatever's wrong?

DR.CAR: Of course. That's why they call me the doctor.

DAD (Sighs): Oh good. You had me worried.

DR.CAR: She'll have to stay here a few days, but I think she'll be running as good as new when she's done.

DAD: It's gonna be hard to manage without her.

DR.CAR: I know it's an inconvenience, but won't it be worth it to have her back almost as good as when you first got her?

DAD: Wow! You can do that?

DR.CAR: That's why they call me the doctor. But listen, don't you want to know how much this is all gonna cost?

DAD: She's the most important thing in my life right now. I don't care how much it costs. It has to be done, right?

DR.CAR: If you wanna get any more mileage out of her.

DAD: Go ahead then.

DR.CAR: You know Mr. Robinson, I hope I'm not overstepping my boundaries here, but from the look of things someone's been running her awfully hard. She won't be long for this world if you don't take better care of her. Pamper her a little bit more. Fill 'er up with the good stuff. I know it costs a little bit more, but she won't complain so much going up hills. It'll keep her running smoother. Not so many knocks and pings.

DAD: She really has been starting to complain lately, especially in the morning until she gets going.

DR.CAR: You'll notice it most on those cold mornings. Do you have something to cover her with?

DAD: A blanket?

DR.CAR: Do you have one big enough? That's great.

DAD: I beg your pardon?!

DR.CAR: Start keeping her on a regular maintenance schedule and she may last you another four or five years.

DAD: That's all?

DR.CAR: Well, you can always get a new one or a slightly used one in good condition if she goes.

DAD: I happen to be very happy with the one I have.

DR.CAR: Then I suggest you appreciate her, don't run her so hard, and make sure she gets regular check-ups.

DAD: Yes, doctor. I'll do that.

DR.CAR: Call me Gary.

DAD: Fine then, Gary. I'll tell my wife what you've said.

DR.CAR: Okey, dokey, then. Will do. Bye.

DAD: Good bye. [Hangs up phone] Poor Helen. I've been working her too hard, expecting too much from her lately. No wonder she's tired. [Helen enters.] Helen! You're back?

MOM: I forgot my phone. [Picks up cellphone] I can't do this. There's no way I can make my dentist appointment and Stephen's practice. I gotta cancel my appointment.

DAD: No! No! No! Don't do that. You need to take good care of yourself. Where's Stephen?

MOM: They're both out in the van. Tim should be unconscious by now.

DAD: Look it. Let me drop them off at practice. When's your appointment?

MOM: In 10 minutes. The practice starts at 4:30.

DAD: Okay. I'll drop you off first. Get the boys where they're going and then pick you up and… take you out for dinner? Wherever you want to go.

MOM: Something wrong, Ted?

DAD: No nothing… um… why?

MOM: Well I don't know. Come on let's go then… [Moves towards exit]

DAD: Um… Your doctor called.

MOM [Turns back]: My doctor?

DAD: Yeah… Dr. Carr.

MOM: Oh… my doctor… uh, huh? Um… what did he say?

DAD [Gets close to her]: I'm sorry Helen. I've been taking you for granted. You've been working too hard. From now on I want you to start taking it easier, okay? [Crosses in front of her, leans offstage and yells to boys in the van] Hey, you two knock it off! [Turns back to Helen] I'm gonna start taking care of you. You need a break. Would you like a day off? How 'bout Mondays? [Exits]

MOM (To self): Good ol' Dr. Car. [Exits]

[BLACKOUT]

Have you ever had one of those thousand-year-like days, or a season of life even, that is so exhausting that when you hear the word "rest" it brings you to tears? It's especially so for me when I hear Matthew 11:28-29, where Jesus says, "Come to Me all you who are weary and burdened and I will give you rest. Take My yoke upon you and learn from Me, for I am gentle and humble in heart and you will find rest for your souls." Rest for my soul? Is that even possible? All I know is that it sounds so good, I cry.

When I'm so totally exhausted that I've forgotten how to rest, resting actually sounds like work. Honestly, I think there are times I'm afraid that if I were to stop, I'd never be able to start again. How'd I get here? All the plates were spinning high in the air on their little bendy sticks and the audience was cheering me on and telling me how amazing it was that I could keep them all balanced and spinning at the same time. But then it went from being amazing to being expected, and then actually being demanded of me to prove my worth. If just one plate teeters or topples, I'll be booed off the stage. Not just humbled… humiliated, demoted, thought less of.

In the world of plate spinning and multitasking, taking a break is not only thought of as a sign of weakness but as potentially catastrophic. It's a mindset that can drive you crazy. It already feels like such a crazy time to be alive. So fast. So demanding. So "pretend-reality-ish." So dark. I'm sure life has felt pretty unreal to every person throughout history no matter what century, but I'm in THIS one, so it feels worse. I think it has something to do with being spiritual beings in physical bodies, meant for eternity, but stuck in time. We were originally created to be unlimited, tireless, unstoppable, but now, because of the fall of man (our decision to try to live independently of

God) we are being trained and prepared for eternity by living in bodies that require us to rest and surrender to our Creator for tune-ups and recalibrations. Try to change the oil while the car is still moving or drive through the gas station without stopping for gas, and eventually the car will commit mutiny, and stop FOR you.

"To Dance"

My soul is sighing, I got nothing left to pour.
My heart is lying and telling me it's sure, "I gotta do this alone."
Though it never worked before, I gotta, just gotta keep on trying.

My soul is crying and only God knows why.
My heart keeps trying to maybe once before I die, find it's rhythm,
The one to finally satisfy my need, my need to be dancing.

Looks like miles before I sleep, running from something I can't see.
Can't go back and yet I can't go on. Never has pavement felt so hard,
So alone, and I'm so tired. And the light of day is almost gone,
But all I know is I hafta keep running.

My soul is dying. It never seemed to have a chance.
My heart's denying that it needs to be romanced.
I can't do this alone, but I don't know how to dance.
Will you please, please could you show me?

Your song calls my soul, Your love woos my heart.
Your lyrics cry out my name. But still I gotta run.
This river runs too deep. Won't someone please ask me again?
Ask me again.

Looks like miles before I sleep, running from something I can't see.
Can't go back and yet I can't go on. Never has pavement felt so hard,
So alone, and I'm so tired. And the light of day is almost gone,
But all I know is I hafta stop my running.
To dance, I know I hafta stop my running.
I know to dance, I hafta stop.

You can ignore the check engine light and convince yourself that it's just a malfunctioning sensor, but when that engine light starts flashing, do yourself and everyone on the road with you a favor — pull over and STOP THE CAR!

Do we think any less of a driver because he stops to get gas or change the oil or have the front end realigned? Do we think of them as weak or inferior people? Do we think a car is a piece of junk because it needs routine maintenance to operate smoothly? Where did we get this idea that the more we do without stopping or resting, the more worth and value we have as people? Does perseverance through abusive situations for applause or approval build character? Is love really gained by spreading yourself in so many directions that the dreaded disappointment or disapproval from others (that you were desperately trying to avoid) inevitably comes crashing in on you?

I know when the word "rest" makes me cry, I'm seconds away from the engine light flashing. I'm not spinning plates, I've become one, and God wants to gracefully dethrone me, catch me, and save me from shattering. He wants to save me... from myself.

I think what He's showing me is that rest is a mindset. If our souls are comprised of mind, will, and emotions, rest for my soul is peace of mind, surrender of my will, and healing of my emotions. Since repentance is literally a change of mind and His kindness leads me to repentance, "Come to Me all you who are weary and find rest for your souls," is really Jesus' kind invitation to come rethink priorities so He can give new perspective, take stress away, and soothe any heartache I'm carrying. He'll teach me how to tread through life while He bears the brunt of the burden (the yoke) and walks alongside me. All I have to do is close my eyes and see His smile, feel His grace, lean into His strong shoulder, and know that I'm loved, I'm okay. His yoke is easy. I'm being restored. He is kind in all His ways and only has good plans for me. Don't look back anymore. Know what you know and face forward. Then I open one eye, "Am I resting yet?"

"Those Were the Days"

SCENE: Two adult actors portraying kids, sitting center stage in oversized-chairs to make them look smaller.

[LIGHTS UP]

BRAD: So... whaddya wanna do?

JOANNE: I dunno. Whaddya you wanna do?

BRAD: I dunno... Hey! How about playdough?

JOANNE: No, you always eat it.

BRAD: Do not.

JOANNE: There's always some missing when we're done.

BRAD: Well, only the green kind.

JOANNE: See, told ya.

BRAD: I promise I won't eat any.

JOANNE: Nah... I don't feel like playing playdough.

BRAD: How 'bout video games?

JOANNE: It's broken.

BRAD: What? Oh!

JOANNE: Hey, maybe we could play "House."

BRAD: House?

JOANNE: That's what my mom says they did when she was a kid. Before video games a kid had to use her 'magination. She says if her favorite TV show wasn't on, she had to color or play a game or pretend. They used to play "House."

BRAD: Okay... I'll be the window [Stands up and sits down repeatedly saying] Open... closed... open... closed.

JOANNE: No! Not house, "House!" Like I'm the mommy and you're the daddy and you fixed me a really fancy supper because I got a promotion and that's really good with the bad ick-on-me.

BRAD: Ick on you? Did you spill the fancy supper I cooked?

JOANNE: No! The ick-on-me. You know. No money and stuff and no jobs and everything costs too much.

BRAD: Oh... I know that. I heard my dad say that before... economy. It used to be better, right?

JOANNE: Yeah, before recess.

BRAD: What?

JOANNE: Before they had the recess.

BRAD: Oh... right.

JOANNE: Now cause of recess you can't buy as much stuff.

BRAD: My mom and dad are always talking about when things used to be better.

JOANNE: Yeah? My mom and dad too.

BRAD: Really? I wonder how come.

JOANNE: Maybe everything used to be really, really good or something.

BRAD: Are you gonna eat the fancy supper I made you?

JOANNE: First I hafta take some aspirins 'cause I have a wicked headache. [Mimes taking aspirin and eating] Now we should talk about grown up stuff.

BRAD: Like when things were better.

JOANNE: Yeah.

BRAD: Okay… marember when we didn't have to go to preschool and we could play at home all morning?

JOANNE: Yeah, that was great! And remember when our moms used to tie our shoes for us and we didn't hafta bend over or anything?

BRAD: My mom still does.

JOANNE: But you're almost five!

BRAD: I know.

JOANNE: And you can't tie your shoes?

BRAD: I can… it's just easier if I pretend I can't.

JOANNE: Pretty smart.

BRAD: I know.

JOANNE: Remember the good ol' days before your little sister and my baby brother were born?

BRAD: I can't marember that long ago.

JOANNE: Well, it was a whole lot better, believe me. And remember a long time ago when it was summer and we used to go get ice cream?

BRAD: Yeah! Oh! Oh! Oh! Marember getting push-up pops from the ice cream truck. I love that song it plays. [Hums and la la la's the theme from "The Sting"]

JOANNE (Interrupts): My mom didn't let me get pops from the ice cream truck. She says you can buy practically a whole box at the store for the same money. But it's not the same.

BRAD: My mom says that, too… but my dad lets us get it when my mom's not around.

JOANNE: He's nice.

BRAD: Sometimes… marember when we could fit into the seat at the grocery store, you know, in the cart, and we didn't hafta walk?

JOANNE (Frowning): Yeah, it always used to pinch my bottom.

BRAD: Oh, you're right. And my legs used to fall asleep by the time we were done shopping… never mind marembering when we could fit in the grocery cart seat.

JOANNE: Hey, you know what?

BRAD: What?

JOANNE: Talking about when things were better makes me feel yucky.

BRAD: Me too… I kinda like things now.

JOANNE: Hey… when we grow up, now is gonna be when things were better, right?

BRAD: Yeah, so it must be pretty good now, huh?

JOANNE: You wanna play playdough?

BRAD: I thought you didn't wanna.

JOANNE: We better have all the fun that we can, 'cause if now is gonna be better than "then," then we better make now really, really good so "then" will be better than if now wasn't as good.

BRAD (Confused): Okay, I'll play playdough.

JOANNE: We hafta play with it in the kitchen.

BRAD: Okay. [Exiting] I get the green!

[BLACKOUT]

Bring with you the lessons, the feelings, the courage, and strength gained from yesterday's workout. Don't try and recreate the beautiful moments of the good ol' days because what's coming is so much better that those moments will just pale in comparison. No worries, no regrets. No listening to the harassments of used-to-be, could've been, what if, and (the loudest one for me) don't even think about closing your eyes until you figure this all out.

There is nothing that surprises or confounds God. Everything that looms before us, stands below and behind Him. He's hidden treasures for us to discover, some of them in scary places and behind situations that confuse us or make us uncomfortable so that we have to trust Him and follow His lead. But He always turns the Light on for us as we rest in His presence. To override the harassments, focus on His presence, and let the world spin all it wants.

Turn your eyes upon Jesus. Look full in His wonderful Face
And the things of earth will grow strangely dim
In the Light of His Glory and Grace.[3]

Rest in His unexplainable grace. No need to figure it out.

I'm so glad that I don't have to figure ANYTHING out. It is what it is, and only if I choose to engage will it be mine to try to understand, or at least to think I understand... [Deep breath, exhale, long pause] Wait! What was that? For about ten seconds just now, it felt like… was that rest? I think I just experienced Sabbath rest. I need to try that again. But how'd I do it? It started with the thought, "I don't have to figure anything out." My soul, tired from trying so hard to figure out how to stop trying so hard, unexpectedly jumped into a state of "wow-how-did-I-get-here?" rest. It was almost like sleeping, but consciously. It wasn't about quieting my heart and shutting out the voices this time. It was more about "NOT doing." Knowing that Jesus is sovereign and all-knowing and has EVERYTHING figured out, makes it possible for me to be still while the world spins around me, just letting Him be the Savior of it all. I don't have to do a thing right now.

---

[3] Helen H. Lemmel, 1922.

God never expects us to do anything He doesn't give us the tools and abilities to do (or not do). He created us to create and enjoy the work of our hands, as He enjoys with us what we are able to do. Not to impress others with our talent, but to create and work and do, like we are doing it for Him to enjoy — as to the Lord, not for men (Colossians 3:23). He designed us to get energy from doing what we love to do. But to keep us on track, to give our souls a rest, and give Him a chance to recalibrate and align us, He tells us to take one out of seven days to rest from "the doing," and let Him pour back into us what we're depleted of, before body and soul run out of gas.

Even if you love your work and time flies while you labor, a day away from it keeps you from being consumed by it. But rest comes down to trusting — trusting that the world will go on, nothing will collapse, and no one on this planet will leave it, just because you don't show up for one day. I actually wrote down one morning:

If I don't show up today will the day still happen? Do I have to bring something to this day that no one else can bring? What is it that needs to be changed today? Me or something out there? What kind of change would my presence bring, or would my lack of presence actually bring the change needed?

Is this a day of refreshing for me? A day for You to straighten, strengthen, and tuck me back in? I got tousled around yesterday. My thoughts got yanked and stepped on. You stepped in and stopped any damage. Thank You! There's more life to come, to overcome, and to take in and smile about. It's amazing how in the middle of all this You inject unexplainable peace.

To watch the effects of Your restoration process is fascinating. I feel like my job, so many times, is to whisper to my friends, "Hold still. Just a minute more. He's doing something awesome. You're going to be unstoppable when He's done." Thank You for putting others in my life who will whisper the same to me.

Rest equals Trust. But that means for those of us who have a hard time trusting, rest can be work. Even though God has given us our tools and talents with which to work, they're the very things we need to lay down and surrender to Him once a week. Then we can come to Him undistracted and learn of Him, get re-yoked to His strength, follow His lead, and find that "how'd-I-get-here" rest for our souls.

Rest is part of following the Shepherd — to lie down in green pastures and be led by still waters and have our souls restored. So, what are you waiting for? How about a personal invitation? If you're a follower of Jesus, He extends an invitation in Mark 6:31 to you:

*"Come with Me by yourselves to a
quiet place and get some rest."*

Now there's an offer that we just can't afford to refuse!

Chapter 9: M.A.S.H.E.D. /COMMUNITY

SCENE: Two men in an Army kitchen, sitting on stools, peeling potatoes.

[LIGHTS UP]

BRAD: I still don't get it.

TIM: Get what?

BRAD: What's the big deal? So I didn't tuck in one little corner of my bunk. I never even pulled up the covers when I was at home.

TIM (Hums or whistles): "You're in the Army Now."

BRAD: Yeah, right. (Mutters) "You're in the Army Now." (Louder) Don't remind me. A whole 37 hours and 15 minutes of being all that I can be. Look how far it's gotten me. Ordinary civilian to master 1st class potato peeler in less than two days. I didn't think they actually did this anymore.

TIM: What? Peel potatoes?

BRAD: Yeah. I thought that was a fifties kind of thing. Like on some old black and white TV show.

TIM: Well, welcome to the real world.

BRAD: This isn't the real world. The real world is out there. This feels more like a bazaar sitcom. I expect Gomer Pyle to pop around the corner any minute and start singing "Impossible Dream."

TIM: Hey at least you don't have Seargent Carter breathing down your neck.

BRAD: I got worse. Some bozo named Furley.

TIM: Really? Furley?

BRAD: He has this warped idea that I have an attitude. He's the one with the problem. He gets his kicks from kicking everybody else around. I'd like to kick him... (Trails off)

TIM: A lot of good that would do you. You'd end up right back here.

BRAD: Yeah, it might just be worth it though. I thought my father was a loser until I met this... (Censors himself) guy... Figures, I have my father to thank for all this. He was the one who "insisted" I join the Army in the first place. He just didn't wanna pay my college tuition. Some dad he turned out to be.

TIM: It's Father's Day, you know.

BRAD: You're kidding. Today? You keep track of these things?

TIM: I have a little girl at home. A baby girl three months old.

BRAD (Sarcastically): Lucky you.

TIM: This is my first Father's Day.

BRAD: Well, Happy Father's Day, Dad. And such a memorable one, huh? Peeling potatoes.

TIM: Yeah, it stinks!

BRAD: So what did you do to pull KP duty?

TIM: My sergeant told me to give him ten I and hesitated.

BRAD: Aw! Crime of the century. You hesitated! Furley would have thrown you in the brig!

TIM: You just don't get this, do you?

BRAD: What, and you do?

TIM: The sergeant's job is to train men into becoming soldiers.

BRAD: [Holds up peeler] Training us to use secret weapons of "mashed" destruction? What are we, vegetable patrol?

TIM: This is boot camp. It's to get us ready for warfare. Furley's not the enemy. He's just trying to get you ready to face the real enemy. Somebody that wants to kill you. You were kind of right when you said this isn't the real world. In the real world my hesitation could have cost somebody's life.

BRAD: And the untucked corner of my bunk?

TIM: Paying attention to detailed orders and obeying for obedience sake, even when you don't understand, is the only way to survive on the battlefield. Your untucked corner, in the real world, could have given away a plan of attack or made you a casualty of war.

BRAD (Pause): I guess you have a point... and what makes you so wise?

TIM: I dunno. Maybe it's because I'm a father.

BRAD: Yeah that must be it. (Pause) I wonder if Furley's somebody's father.

TIM: Yeah, he is.

BRAD: Ha! Who'd marry him?

TIM: My mother.

[BLACKOUT]

It's hard to believe that disobedience, or delayed obedience, could have such an impact on anybody besides ourselves. But when we're living as a community, what we do, or hesitate to do, can really make a big difference to a lot of people. That kind of pressure can make us want to hide under the covers or find a comfy cave somewhere and make it our very own hermitage.

Real community isn't forced. It's coaxed and nurtured and sometimes spontaneous altogether. It has been designed to bring God pleasure. It makes Him so happy to see us get along. Think about how fun it is for us to watch animals chase and play and groom each other. It reflects community. We're heartened by the idea of penguins working together, sacrificing for one another, protecting each other. We like seeing prides of lions standing strong together, hunting, wrestling playfully, and defending each other, and even sharing the catch of the day. That's community.

Can you imagine how God feels to see us loving and caring for each other, laughing and crying together, working, defending, and sacrificing for one another — to be in relationship and community by choice and doing what He designed us to do? How satisfying that must be for Him.

Wouldn't it make sense for God's enemy, the devil, who works so hard to divide and conquer God's image-bearers, to attack us by trying to isolate and expose us one by one, drawing us each away from the safety and community of our herd? Besides his old stand-by strategy, to cause confusion and offense by miscommunication (injecting lies and doubt into our minds as we converse), a subtle and not as easily detected way was introduced back in the early 1990's under the guise of "better" communication technology.

Without doing a word study, I can still confidently guess that communication and community come from the same root words (I'll let you Google it). I wrote the following sketch in 1994 when automation began creeping into our everyday lives and we had started to feel the effects. I had no idea that what was being sown by the enemy back then would grow and blossom into the huge plastic family tree, complete with wax fruit, that we call "community" today. Here's how it started:

"Automated Religion"

SCENE: A room in a house. Husband sitting at computer.

[LIGHTS UP]

WIFE: [Enters furious] I can't believe it! It ate my card!

HUSBAND (Stares at computer and talks in a daze): Hi Honey, how's your day?

WIFE: I knew as soon as I drove up to that automated teller, I could tell just by the way it was flashing those silly credit card pictures at me, I didn't stand a chance.

HUSBAND: That's good, what's for supper?

WIFE: Someone had ripped off the receiver to the service phone, just the cord was hanging there. There was nobody to help me. Nobody to complain to.

HUSBAND: Uh huh.

WIFE: That cold steely machine chomped up my card, the card with my name on it, into little bitty pieces.

HUSBAND: You don't say.

WIFE: I hate all those machines. Everywhere you go. No more real people waiting to help you. [Looks at him] Just a screen with buttons.

HUSBAND: Buttons, uh huh.

WIFE (Over husband's shoulder): And when certain weak-minded people sit in front of them, they almost meld together with the machine. Mindless. Oblivious to the needs of their wife.

HUSBAND: I know. It's awful, isn't it?

WIFE: [Hits him and gets his attention] You don't even care, you haven't heard a thing.

HUSBAND: I heard. It's just I was almost to level four.

WIFE: What'd I say?

HUSBAND: You said... um... hey! You never answered my question. What's for supper?

WIFE: I couldn't pick up supper because the ATM ate my card and I couldn't get any money to pay for it.

HUSBAND: Did you use the little service phone?

WIFE: Oh, just forget it!

HUSBAND: That's what they're there for, you know.

WIFE: I just wish that instead of all these machines and recordings, you could deal with a person once in a while. Our parents would have had a warm friendly teller handing them their money instead of a machine spitting it out or gobbling it up.

HUSBAND: We'll take care of it Monday, okay?

WIFE: Everything is so automated.

HUSBAND: So the banks have ATMs, big deal.

WIFE: Not just the banks. What about gas stations. There's nobody to pump your gas or clean your windshield...

HUSBAND: Did you stop for gas?

WIFE: I didn't have any money and you have the gas card. They don't even need someone to take money. You just put your card in the machine and pray it doesn't eat it.

HUSBAND: Okay, so banks and gas stations are a little less...

WIFE: And toll booths. You can't ask directions from a basket. There's no personal interaction anymore and then there's the doctors... I called the doctor's office the other day to get a refill on your prescription. I got a recording and after pressing all the right buttons, 1 for this and 2 for that, I got to talk to voice mail! I won't know till I go to the pharmacy whether they heard me or not.

HUSBAND: But, Honey (Patronizingly) machines are our friends.

WIFE: Maybe some of your friends are machines. That would explain why they act like they do.

HUSBAND: What about dishwashers, microwaves, driers, washing machines...

WIFE: I'm talking about things that are automatic and cold that should be personal and friendly.

HUSBAND: I think you might be overreacting just a...

WIFE: Even creditors don't have the decency to yell at you anymore. They let the computer do the dialing and a recording do the scolding.

[Telephone rings]

HUSBAND: Speaking of which...

WIFE: Probably some sales pitch. It's suppertime, right?

HUSBAND: Let the machine get it.

WIFE: Okay.

HUSBAND: See, impersonal automated telephone receptionists come in handy sometimes.

WIFE: Shhh, I want to hear.

RECORDING: (Wife's voice): "We can't come to the phone right now, but please leave your name and number and we'll get back to you as soon as we can. Have a good day." RECORDED WOMAN'S VOICE: Hold the line please. We have an important recorded message just for you. (Pause)

WIFE: See what I mean.

RECORDING CONTINUES (MAN'S VOICE): Hello folks. Don't hang up your phone. Your eternity depends on it! I'm the friendly Reverend Frank Snurdly from the First Community Church of the Holy Hug, and we're calling to invite you to join us this Sunday for a time you won't be able to forget. You can't afford to miss meeting our warm friendly holy-hugging congregation here at First Community. We're here to meet all your needs. [Pause]

[Wife gets up to hang up the phone.]

RECORDING CONTINUES (MAN'S VOICE): Wait there's more. Need some prayer? Call our number and press 1. Each day you get to hear a new inspiring dial-a-prayer message. Want to learn more about the Bible? Press 2 to start receiving your absolutely free "Bible at Your Fingertips" correspondence course. Your love gift of $50.00 or more will ensure that these free courses will continue to come in a timely fashion. And remember, God loves a cheerful giver so give us all you've got. Press 3 when you call us to find out where to send your generous tithes and offerings. Press 4 if you want to sign up to clean the church on a weekly basis and 5 if you need to leave a message for the pastor. Someone will return your call just as soon as possible, unless it's the weekend. Remember, we here at First Community Church care about you, whoever you are. So give us a call at 1-555... [Wife picks up receiver and hangs it up to disconnect it.]

WIFE: Can you stand it? Even religion is automated! What next? What in the world is next?!

HUSBAND: Come on, it's not all that bad... all that bad (Like computerized tick) all that bad... [Wife hits husband with a pillow.]

[BLACKOUT]

The next step was to make those cold steely machines seem more friendly and personal. As technology advanced, so did the need to make soulless machines sound like real, live, friendly, always polite people who actually care — the kind of voice you can trust to guide you home when you're totally lost, and one that will always sound calm and reassuring even while "she" navigates you gently down a boat ramp into the lake recalculating glub... glub... glub.

Then we needed a friendly cheerful voice that actually responds to our voice commands over the phone, no matter how aggressive your voice may get after waiting hours listening to how important you are and how sorry she is and how the next available representative will be with you shortly. And then, because of sheer repetition when you finally start believing her and respond in a calm rational voice, she simply says, "Sorry, I didn't quite get that. Please call again. Goodbye."

We are placed into families as a way of preparing us to navigate through life in community. Some are blessed into families that represent God's original intent. Others are, instead, born into situations that teach them how to survive community. Being surrounded by broken people who don't know Jesus, always bumping into each other, getting in each other's way, can make living in community feel more like punishment. But no matter where you may find yourself in the first community experience spectrum, the attractiveness of gentle, polite voices (even if automated) and cyber relationships that require little maintenance, can be very alluring. Convenient friends you can choose to respond to or simply ignore, that you can throw an emoji at or "unfriend" with a click of a mouse (no confrontation required), and always being able to put your best foot forward with your good side toward the camera, have made us forget the better or worse part, the iron-sharpens-iron side of true community. Like a live vaccine builds up our immunity to the actual disease, the health benefits of true community caused by face to face conflict, disagreements, compromise, submission, and sacrifice of time have been lost to more comfortable, convenient, rehearsed conversations. Defending, sacrificing, and wrestling with (the very things that move us when we watch animals interact) are lost in technology.

Don't get me wrong, I really do appreciate the amazing avenues of communication and information opened to us through technology. I grew up with encyclopedias, not exactly pocket-sized, so to have accessibility to the latest of the latest info available, minute by minute, is mind boggling to me. I can't quite wrap my head around being able to keep up to date on current events from anywhere and anytime. But here's the downside: you never get to just sit and wonder anymore.

"Searching for answers" has taken on a whole new meaning, and the lessons of patience, diligence, and determination that used to ready you for the ah-ha moment and reward of the answer have all but faded away. In fact, you're apt to find yourself tapping your fingers and sighing in disgust for the few seconds the information requested takes to download. What was once considered "instant" is no longer fast enough.

I'm not against technological advances. I'm only suggesting the personal warmth and true benefits of community have been displaced by more controllable, less demanding online relationships that give the illusion of what God intended for us.

Have you ever been stuck in an elevator with strangers, or all of a sudden found yourself stranded at the airport with new found friends, or outside with neighbors picking up after a bad storm and you're pooling resources, helping each other out, sharing stories, comparing notes, and urging each other forward? When a crisis happens, when there's danger, it's what we're wired to do — to band together, to help each other. We form community.

When there's no crisis, no persecution or common problem, we find it pretty easy to ignore our need to commune, and we convince ourselves it's better to keep to ourselves and not bother anyone, nor be bothered by them. We think we're craving alone time (funny that we can't seem to leave our phone behind) but what I think we're really craving is true intimacy with "real" people.

We've been lulled into thinking that the spiritual battle raging around us is for someone else to fight. The community called "church," once a boot-camp-like training-ground, has now become, for most, purely social, somewhat educational, even sometimes entertaining, but in general, optional. As long as it fits into the schedules of our busy lives and ringing calendar reminders, we'll consider "the gathering together" as doable.

But in so many places around the world, the optional gathering together we call "going to church" is a matter of survival. It is a death-defying choice that persecuted people make every time they gather and yet they consider it pure joy. Carrying your cross is not about wearing your necklace secretly under your shirt because it's not permitted at work. It's about risking your life to tell someone at work Jesus loves them and died for them so they can be in right relationship with their Creator and Heavenly Father. Even if they die a martyr's death, they will live on. If they are tortured, as you have been, you can assure them that God will grace them through. That's carrying your cross daily.

Just as I started writing this chapter, I heard God say, "Hebrews 13:3." This is what I read, "Remember those in prison as though you were their fellow prisoners, and those who are mistreated as if you yourself were suffering." Was God talking to me about those I love who are in spiritual bondage? Then that night, a preacher quoted Hebrews 13:3 when talking about fellow Christians around the world today who are suffering persecution, torture, crucifixion, and beheading. The next day, a gentleman I prayed for told me about a movement of prayer for persecuted Christians. At 8:38 PM ET, people around the world are lifting up those in prison and those being mistreated for Jesus' Name sake. And I thought, "That's my community."

As much as we are connected and able to communicate easily all around the world, how often do we in the Western Church suffer in our spirits with our persecuted community family members? We may not have met them yet, but we know in our hearts they are there. We can feel it. We hear of their suffering and persecution, and yet we find something in our own circumstances to justify ourselves and we look for something in our own experience of "church community" to pathetically complain about as excuses for isolating: "The sermon is too long. The people are so hypocritical. There's too much gossip there. The music is so loud. Nobody bothers to talk to me. I don't think anyone would miss me if I didn't go. Maybe I'll just stay home and stream it. Then I won't have to deal with all that other stuff. Better yet, I'll wait till later and then I can skip the singing part and listen to a shortened version of the sermon. I won't have to put anything in the offering plate and I'll be saving money on gas by not driving there. That's just being a good steward."

It's not to imply that true community can only be found in a church building or that the way most people I know "do church" is even conducive to true community. In fact, any church of considerable size in our neck of the woods will tell you that one of their main goals, and often their biggest struggle, is to get people to meet in smaller "community groups" during the week. Why is it so hard? Ever notice how the word community ends in "unity"? It suggests intimacy, honesty, vulnerability, and trust. For most of us these days, those words sound scary. But it's what we're made for. It's how we thrive.

If a naturally wild animal that belongs to a herd, flock, pride, or pod was brought into captivity and isolated, it wouldn't be surprising to see signs of depression, lethargy, or aggression develop, or even a shortened life span as a result. How much more, when we find ourselves isolated, ostracized, shunned, or separated, will we suffer at a deep spiritual level? Have you noticed an increase of anxiety, depression, and suicide? Yes, the days are dark, but do you think they're any darker than, let's say, the Dark Ages? You were created for family, relationships, community, and physical hugs (not just emojis of a bear hugging itself or blowing kisses).

We need to experience the comradery of the disciples, catching the quick nods of encouragement from each other across an angry crowd, or the looks of amazement as we watch baskets of food multiply in our hands and we shrug from across the field, "Is this really happening? I'm not crazy, right? It's happening over there too?" These guys practically lived together for three years of boot camp. Interesting that boot camp is never for an army of one. Only in community, with each of us together reflecting back to God the facets of Him we were designed to reflect, can we blind the enemy with the magnitude needed, as we magnify the Light and Glory of Jesus, altogether... as one.

"Home Stretch"

SCENE: Two racers meet alongside the Columbus Day race course. Trees and a park bench are nearby.

[LIGHTS UP]

BRAD: [Enters winded] I can't do this. I just... can't. This is far enough.

TIM: [Enters jogging wearily] You okay?

BRAD: Not really.

TIM: You need a medic?

BRAD: No, a psychologist. What was I thinking? I can't believe I actually thought that I could run this far.

TIM: But you did run this far. We both did.

BRAD: I think I just need to sit down.

TIM: No, don't do that. You're supposed to keep moving. I learned this from my dad. He used to run this Columbus Day race all the time. He even won a few times. Now it's my turn.

BRAD: I hate to tell you, but I don't think you're gonna win.

TIM: Oh, I know. But hey, I'm giving it my best shot. At least I'm trying anyhow. Come on, we're almost there.

BRAD: [Starts to follow] I think this is far enough, don't you? I can't run another step. [Sits down on park bench]

TIM: Who says we hafta run?

BRAD: It's a race remember? We're supposed to run across the finish line.

TIM: Nothing says you hafta run. Just finish.

BRAD: Okay, I'm finished.

TIM: No, come on, we hafta cross the finish line. [Pulls Brad up]

BRAD: [Draws line with foot] Well this is my finish line. [Steps over it] There I crossed it.

TIM: That doesn't count. The judge says the finish line is down the road.

BRAD: Ah, what does the judge know? I want it to be here, right now, right here! This is the line and I crossed it.

TIM: Aw, come on now. Think of all your hard training.

BRAD: You could tell I trained?

TIM: Sure, you got this far. You had to have worked hard.

BRAD: Right. Hard enough and now it's time for a vacation.

TIM: Ask yourself, "Why did I enter this race?"

BRAD: That's JUST what I've been asking myself.

TIM: Come on, why did you start running?

BRAD: I dunno, I guess… I liked the challenge of it.

TIM: Good, there you go.

BRAD: But I had no idea when I started this race I'd be in this much pain by the end.

TIM: But that IS the challenge of running. Enduring the pain. Enduring it all the way to victory.

BRAD: Victory? We're gonna be the last ones to cross the finish line.

TIM: Victory isn't winning the race; it's winning the battle.

BRAD: You should put that on a bumper sticker or something. Victory isn't winning the race it's... what?

TIM: Winning the battle.

BRAD: Yeah, right. That's really good. [Pause] So how come you entered the race?

TIM: It's Columbus Day. I'm doing it for my dad.

BRAD: Is he waiting at the finish line for you?

TIM: You could say that... he died a few months ago.

BRAD: Oh, I'm sorry.

TIM: He had his own battle. But he was a real runner, you know? A real athlete. He didn't quit before he crossed the finish line. So I'm running for him. Well maybe not running, but at least I'm gonna finish it for him... I better get going. The parade's gonna come through here pretty soon. [Starts to walk away]

BRAD: Hey number 5!

TIM: Yeah?

BRAD: I'll race ya?

TIM: You're on!

[They walk and limp down through the audience.]

BRAD: I wonder if this is what they mean by slow and steady wins the race.

[BLACKOUT]

Chapter 9: M.A.S.H.E.D. /COMMUNITY

Chapter 10: How Do You Spell Belief?

SCENE: All parts onstage are played by two actors. They stand with their backs to the audience when not talking. A coat rack full of costume props stands between them. When it's the actor's turn to talk, their character turns and faces the audience, steps forward and says their lines. When they're done, they walk back to the coat rack, swap costume props for their next character, and then go back and freeze in place with their back to the audience (till it's their turn to talk again). The lines of the "Voice" are spoken from offstage over the sound system.

[LIGHTS UP]

VOICE: How do you spell "belief?"

OLD WOMAN: C-H-U-R-C-H! That pretty much spells it, don't you think? Going to church is practicing your faith. It's the main focus of religion itself. C-H-U-R-C-H.

TEENAGER: P-A-R-E-N-T-S! I don't have much choice but to believe the way my parents do. If I question anything, I'll have my curfew shortened. Yeah! I spell belief P-A-R-E-N-T-S!

VOICE: How do you spell "belief?"

TEACHER: If you turn in your spelling books to page 105, you'll see that belief is spelled E-D-U-C-A-T-I-O-N! Education is the key that unlocks life's hidden meaning. If you have a good education, you've got everything!

HIPPIE: Hey man like W-H-A-T-E-V-E-R! Whatever feels good, man. Like, there's no true religion. It's all okay. As long as it feels good. Yeah, whatever.

VOICE: How do you spell "belief?"

MODEL: F-A-S-H-I-O-N! Dress smart and you are smart. Fashion faux pas? (Wagging finger) Tsk! Tsk! Tsk! No one will like you. Coordinate your wardrobe religiously and attain that sense of dressed for success happiness!

VOICE: How do you spell "belief?"

SERGEANT: I can't hear you!

VOICE (Louder): How do you spell "belief?"

SERGEANT: I still can't hear you!

VOICE: How do you spell "belief," Sir?

SERGEANT: That's better. I spell it R-U-L-E-S! Got it? Obey the rules! Don't you ever step out of line, soldier! One mistake and you're on the ground giving me ten. Got that! In my platoon you gotta be all that you can be. Follow my R-U-L-E-S and you might be good enough to get by.

BUSINESS PERSON: Belief? P-O-W-E-R! There's nothing else in life worth living for. Power is what counts. You gotta take charge of your life and everybody else's while you're at it. Don't let anything or anybody stand in your way. And don't let 'em tell you that you can't. Just go for it! Grab ALL the P-O-W-E-R, power!

VOICE: How do you spell "belief?"

FARMER: How do you spell "belief?" None of your B-U-S-I-N-E-S-S! Our religion is our business and we don't have to tell you nothin'!

VOICE: But…

FARMER: We're not sayin' another word!

VOICE: But…

DAUGHTER: Not another word!

VOICE: How do you spell "belief?"

[BLACKOUT]

What's with all the boot camp, warfare, and battle lingo anyway? You'd think we were at war or something. I mean, "Onward Christian soldiers" (really?) "marching as to war"? I like marching tunes as much as any parade goer, but if Jesus was such a peace-loving Man, and we're following in His footsteps, shouldn't we be talking the talk of love, not war?

You can try and convince yourself otherwise (I know I have) and deny all the obvious symptoms and voices in your head. But even TV cartoons will tell you, with an angel on one shoulder and a devil on the other, that there are forces at odds all around us and often times within us. Whether you think it's just a metaphor or not, we are at war. I believe, because of what the Bible teaches, that it's a cosmic war and mankind's allegiance is at the center of disputed territory.

Honestly, I don't like being in the middle of a cosmic war any more than you do. We didn't sign up for this. We were drafted. Even before we were born, we were already drafted. The only choice we get is with which side we want to align ourselves. Actually, it's more like we decide if we want to defect to the winning side or stay where we are.

We were born with our souls tuned into this one propaganda network which 24/7 tries to convince us that "good is bad, bad is good, and possibly, if you meditate long enough, you'll be enlightened to see that maybe there really is no difference between the two because it's all relative." Or is it?

"Splitting Hairs"

SCENE: Inside the second pig's house made of sticks, from the Fairy Tale Classic: *The Three Little Pigs*. Marvin, a pig, is standing center stage with arms crossed.

[LIGHTS UP]

ED: [From off stage shaking the door] Marvin, come on, it's me. LET ME IN!!!!

MARVIN: Not by the hairs on my chinny chin chin.

ED: Marvin, I'm your brother. The Big Bad Wolf just blew my straw house down again and he's headed this way. Come on, Marv! We've done this a hundred times. This is the part where you let me in.

MARVIN: I'm adding a little suspense to the storyline.

ED: This is no time to turn into Steven Spielberg. Open the door!

MARVIN: You've gotta admit, it's making the outcome less predictable.

ED: You're nuts! I'm outta here! I'm going to Bob's house. That's where we always end up anyhow. You'll just hafta stand up to the wolf on your own. See ya!

MARVIN: [Opens door] No wait. Don't do that. Then you'll be admitting that our brother has something we don't.

ED: [Out of breath, shuts door and holds it] What were you thinking? I could have been killed out there.

MARVIN: I was just trying to keep the adventure alive.

ED: By giving me a heart attack? My whole life flashed before my eyes.

MARVIN: It's important to reevaluate and take inventory of your life now and then.

ED: You've been watching Oprah again haven't you?

MARVIN: Actually, I was reading *Pig Quarterly*.

ED: *P.Q.?*

MARVIN: They had one of those "Is Your Life in a Rut?" surveys.

ED: And yours is in a rut?

MARVIN: Ours is in a rut. It's so predictable. We build our houses, yours out of straw, mine out of sticks, the wolf blooooows 'em down, we go to Bob's, we collect the insurance, we build again. We gotta break out. We gotta reset our course.

ED: I kinda like things predictable. No surprises. No unexpected crises. No being left outside to be eaten by a wolf.

MARVIN: You're gonna end up just like Bob.

ED: So? Is that so bad?

MARVIN: You wanna be known as a brick-laying, thinking ahead, always prepared, fuddy-duddy swine-pig?

ED: What's wrong with that?

MARVIN: Ed, come on. Get with it! It's the dawn of a new age! Time to branch out! Discover your true colors. Don't conform to the old standards. It's time to set your own new ones. JUST DO IT!

ED: *P.Q.?*

MARVIN: NIKE®. Question authority! Create your own destiny! Oprah says, "Think for yourself."

ED: You're not thinking for yourself.

MARVIN: I most certainly am.

ED: You're listening to the commercials and magazines and talk shows.

MARVIN: But they're telling me to take charge of my life and don't listen to anybody else.

ED: But you're listening to them.

MARVIN: I guess you're just not as together a pig as I am.

ED: Enough liberated pig talk. Get your coat on. The Big Bad Wolf is gonna be here any second.

MARVIN: And that's another thing.

ED: What, does a coat conform to some archaic dress code or something?

MARVIN: No, the wolf. We know he's big, but how do we know he's bad?

ED: HE WANTS TO EAT US, MARVIN! I know it's the dawn of a new age but being eaten is still a bad thing. Am I right?

MARVIN: How do you know he wants to eat us? All he ever says is, "Little pigs, little pigs let me in." He doesn't say, "Little pigs, little pigs, I wanna eat you."

ED: Now wait a minute. You can't be serious. You're not actually thinking of letting him in, are you?

MARVIN: Well, think of it, Ed. If we let him in, he won't huff and puff and blooooow our house down. We wouldn't have to rebuild anymore.

ED: Ya got a point there. We wouldn't have to rebuild because we wouldn't need a house. We'd be history, gone, finito. We'd be lunch.

MARVIN (Tsk, tsk): Ed, Ed, Ed, Ed, Ed, you need to be more tolerant of wolves. They have feelings and rights, too, you know. It's not their fault they're wolves. They were just born that way.

ED (In disbelief): Where did you hear that one?

MARVIN: The editorial page.

ED: Marvin, there are just some things that don't change with time even though times are changing. Wolves eat pigs whether you are tolerant of them or not. Now, if you are thinking of asking the wolf in for lunch, I am not going to be on the menu. I'm going to Bob's house like I should've done to begin with. I may even ask him for the floor plans to his sturdy, tried-and-true, wolf-proof, brick house. Because you're right about one thing, Marv, I'm sick of rebuilding. If I had only listened to Bob to begin with, I wouldn't have to keep running here because my house would still be standing.
Nice knowin' ya, Marv. [Starts to exit, then sees wolf] Here comes the wolf! I'll use the back door.

MARVIN: There is no back door.

ED: There is now! [Runs through imaginary wall and down through audience]

[Knock at door. Marvin looks at door nervously.]

WOLF: Little pigs, little pigs, let me in!

MARVIN: [Starts to exit out "back door" then stops] Not by the hair... Aw, what does Ed know? How bad could one wolf be? [Starts to open the door, and then freezes]

[BLACKOUT]

How bad could one wolf be? Is "goodness" or "badness" all in our perception? Is truth determined by our personal experiences, or can we learn anything from history and the experience of others?

History has never been a favorite topic of mine. And not being an avid reader, especially of topics I have zero interest in, I found American History to be one of THE most torturous subjects (second only to Algebra) that I had to persevere through in order to graduate high school. Unlike required reading for English assignments, it was almost impossible to guess which facts and characters you had to memorize to fake your way through the test without actually reading the whole chapter. Ugh! And essay questions that you could usually expound on with fluff were not generally part of the final history exam. Add to that a teacher who had no tolerance for any student who didn't share his passion of dead, decaying generals; archaic, bloody battles; and chess-like strategic war games — a teacher who droned on and on about nothing for hours, expecting me to listen with my eyes open and to actually take notes and not doodle — you put it all together and my senior year of high school history class stirs up some pretty pathetic memories for me. So why do I bring it up?

I have a lifelong friend who happened to major in Civil War history and still reads historical documents and generals' memoirs for fun. He can tell you the time, date, circumstances, names, motives, even the weather (and I think probably the direction of the wind and position of the sun) of each and every American Civil War battle. It's absolutely fascinating to watch this usually quiet, soft-spoken man come alive, totally in his element, as he eloquently and passionately describes the victories and losses, ups and downs, grave mistakes, and brilliant strategies of courageous and driven leaders who changed and wrote history with their very lives.

But he had a teacher who impacted his thinking and inspired him greatly, who brought the significance of each battle to life for him. This teacher made history practically touch my friend's soul, and actually influenced how my friend saw life in a new way by studying the lives of brave fighting men from the past. History had changed how this teacher lived his life, and he imparted history's impact to his students. Wow! To have a teacher like that! No wonder my friend loves history!

The truth is, we both went to the same high school and both had the same history teacher.

People can listen to the same person tell the same story, even at the exact same time, but not HEAR the same story at all. I guess it must have something to do with our own personal history and subsequent perspectives on life. But that doesn't change the historical facts, just our understanding of them.

Please bear this in mind as you read the ancient history I am about to write down for you. Now THIS piece of history completely changed my life. But here we are, two different people with different perspectives, so I can only hope it will do the same for you. I especially hope it helps you if this war zone thing feels overwhelming to you. Sorry, you can't just skim over history, but I tried to condense it and include just the parts you need to know for the test. [For the full unedited story, I highly recommend the best history book ever recorded — the Holy Bible.] This is how I see the cosmic war we find ourselves in, and how I've come to terms with the casualties of war I encounter every day. Here goes:

God created the world (actually the universe) to support life for us and then literally gave us the world — to rule, shepherd, nurture, and enjoy. He designed us to live spirit to Spirit in communion with Him forever, to always have access to His pure wisdom so we could be good rulers, loving and just, living in total reliance on Him. So what happened?

The risk God took was to give us a soul, not just our body and spirit. Our soul consists of our *will, emotions,* and *mind*:

Our will gives us the option to choose to trust and obey God, not just be programmed to.
Our emotions let us fall in love with Him, not just love Him automatically.
Our minds receive information from the spiritual realm and transfers it to the physical realm. Our brain signals our body, but our mind signals our brain. Our minds also listen to the will and emotions, while perceiving things in the physical realm and transferring them back to our spirits.

Confused yet? Okay then, like in most history text books I pretended to read, let me make it a little more confusing by adding more words:

When our spirits are out of communion with God's Holy Spirit, we can't help but live from our minds and listen to human reasoning and demonic influence. The accuser, satan, accused us before God day and night. Jesus steps in as our Defense Attorney if we trust Him (see Revelation 12:9-11) but satan has turned to other tactics. He instead accuses us to our faces (in our thoughts) day and night, and lies to us about God, trying to get us to question God's character. He tells us not to worry, we don't need God, that we've got all that we need within us. His goal is to capture our allegiance. That's why satan is considered the enemy. That's why battle lingo is part of our story.

Here's my most recent history lightbulb moment: Fifty years of me knowing Jesus became a Man to die for my sin, and then suddenly it all made sense to me why He had to be a Man. Genesis 1:28 tells us that God ordained that mankind rule this earthly realm, right? So because a man lost that authority to satan (by breaking his covenant with God and trusting satan instead) and because God doesn't renege on something He ordains, it was a Man who had to win that authority back. Jesus, the Son of God, had to become a Son of Man.

Jesus' rescue and recovery mission had to happen both in the physical and spiritual realms because that's how we're made. Blood is both physical and spiritual at the same time. Life is not tangible, but blood is. And life is in the blood. Only by shedding His sinless Blood could Jesus reestablish our covenant with God. Only His perfect life-giving sacrifice could give life back to our spirits, making us righteous to reign again, making us able, once more, to be influenced and empowered by the Holy Spirit — spirit to Spirit in communion with God forever.

One by one, generation to generation, His children's spirits are being raised to life and born again. We are transformed and redeemed as we confess with our physical mouth "Jesus is Lord" and believe in our spiritual heart that God raised Him from the dead. For it is with our heart that we believe and are justified and it is with our mouth that we confess and are saved (see Romans 10:9-10).

"With Ribbons Red"

Your Blood is like a sea of red which parted wide as it was shed.
You made a way. You crossed ahead, and turned to us and said,
"Come follow Me to Higher Ground. I promise you the way is sound.
Though winds and waves are all around, trust Me, you'll not be drowned."
Blood of the Lamb you rescued me, with Ribbons Red that silently
declare Your song of victory. You overwhelm the enemy with Ribbons of Red.

Great drops of Blood that night You cried, a sea of Ribbons deep and wide.
You drown my sins of fear and pride. "Thy Will be done," You sighed.
Then crown of thorns on tender brow. Like Ribbons Red, Love trickled down.
A promise kept. A silent vow to set us free somehow.
Blood of the Lamb you rescued me, with Ribbons Red that silently declare
Your song of victory. You overwhelm the enemy with Ribbons of Red.

Ribbons of Red flow warm and free, streaming Your life abundantly.
You bled a Shield that covers me and makes the darkness flee.

Lamb who was slain, Beloved Son, returns as King, Triumphant One.
Robes dipped in blood; the war is done. Life's song is just begun.
You overwhelmed the enemy with Ribbons Red! You won!
Come, Lord Jesus, come!

With Blood so pure, so strong, erasing every wrong, so now we can belong to You.
Your love sings us a song and we just sing along. Forever we'll sing on to You
...of Ribbons Red.

Someday soon the war will be done, but for now we take heart for Jesus said in this world we will have trouble, but He has overcome the World (see John 16:33). Through the resurrection power of Jesus' Blood that gives life to our once sin-deadened spirits, and cleanses us from all unrighteousness, we have been given the option to switch sides and no longer be under the mastery of sin and satan. Eternal life, in communion again with God's Holy Spirit, can be restored to you by Jesus Himself. And yet for some, this seems so narrow-minded or absurd that they think there just has to be more ways than one to be at peace and to live in freedom with or without God:

"Whatever Works"

SCENE: The stage is split into a living room (where two women, sitting on a sofa, await dinner) and a kitchen (where their boyfriends are trying to create that dinner). Lighting is used to draw the audience's attention from one scene to the other as the dialogue alternates.

[LIGHTS UP ON LIVING ROOM]

JOAN: You sure they don't need help in there?

DARLENE: Let's not spoil the surprise.

JOAN: Brad really thought of this all by himself, huh? Making us dinner like this?

DARLENE: I may have encouraged him a little bit, but yeah, it was mostly his idea.

[Lights down on living room and **LIGHTS UP ON KITCHEN**]

JOE: How'd we get roped into this anyhow?

BRAD: Darlene has been on my case for weeks now. I finally said okay just to keep her quiet.

JOE: But Chinese food?

BRAD: That part was my idea. I figured if we messed it up we could always send out for it and they'd never know.

JOE: Good thinking.

[Lights down on kitchen and **LIGHTS UP ON LIVING ROOM**]

JOAN: I wonder what they're making?

DARLENE: Probably a mess. But it's so sweet of them isn't it? For Valentine's Day?

JOAN: Does Brad cook? 'Cause I know Joe can't.

DARLENE: I'm not sure. But I gave him my foolproof "Even You Can Cook" recipe book. Between the two of them they're sure to come up with something edible.

JOAN: Maybe it would be safer to have them take us out to dinner.

DARLENE: No, Brad wanted this to be special. Nothin' says lovin' like somethin' from the oven.

[LIGHTS UP ON KITCHEN]

BRAD: Maybe we should just take them out somewhere.

JOE: Come on, Brad, we can't do that. I'm broke.

BRAD: That's right, me too. Besides, we're already this far in. [Points to bowl]

JOE: Did you bring ANY ingredients with you?

BRAD: This was Darlene's bright idea. I figured we'd just use what she had in her house.

JOE: Oh, okay… so what else do we need?

BRAD: Let me see here [Looks at book]

[LIGHTS UP ON LIVING ROOM]

JOAN [Picks up book off coffee table.]: What's this?

DARLENE: Oh, it's a book on World Religions. My brother's big into Buddhism now. I thought I'd read up on it before I talked with him.

JOAN: You gonna try to convert him back?

DARLENE: Back to what?

JOAN: Christianity. You're a Christian, right?

DARLENE: Well, I like to think of myself as a little more open-minded than that.

JOAN: You believe in God?

DARLENE: Of course! … among other things.

[LIGHTS UP ON KITCHEN]

JOE: But she doesn't have any soy sauce.

BRAD: What does she have?

JOE: Maple syrup?

BRAD: That's close. I like maple syrup, you?

JOE: Yeah, on pancakes.

BRAD: What about… is there any pork?

JOE: Hot dogs.

BRAD: They're made out of pork. Throw them in.

[LIGHTS UP ON LIVING ROOM]

DARLENE: Have you ever tried Buddhism?

JOAN: Sit around all day worshipping a little statue of some fat bald guy. No Thanks!

DARLENE: That's not Buddhism.

JOAN: Look, I'm gonna stick with Christianity, okay? It's more normal.

DARLENE: But you don't even practice it.

JOAN: I most certainly do to!

DARLENE: Going to church twice a year on Christmas and Easter doesn't qualify as practicing.

JOAN: Well, at least I have a church to go to.

[LIGHTS UP ON KITCHEN]

JOE [Tastes it and spits it out]: This is disgusting.

BRAD (Disbelief): Nooooo. [Tastes it and makes a face] It's just missing something.

JOE: Yeah, edible flavor.

BRAD: Now what would Julia do?

JOE: Julia?

BRAD: Julia Childs. (In a high voice) The key to any good recipe... unlocks the wine cabinet.

JOE: Darlene doesn't have a wine cabinet, does she?

BRAD: Something better. Almond Extract, 80% alcohol [Takes a swig and in a raspy voice] Yup, this should definitely do it.

[LIGHTS UP ON LIVING ROOM]

DARLENE: Don't you see, Joanie? You can take what you like from all the religions out there and make up your own personalized set of beliefs. Religion should be personal, don't you think?

[LIGHTS UP ON KITCHEN]

JOE: I don't know, Brad. This looks pretty disgusting.

BRAD: It can't be. It's everything we like. Hot dogs, maple syrup, garlic powder, Beefaroni, tuna helper, almond extract, and (in a high voice) colorful sprinkles to add that festive holiday flair.

JOE: There's nothing in this pot that's in this recipe.

BRAD: So we substituted a little. How bad could it be?

JOE [Looks again]: Pretty bad.

BRAD: I know! I got it!

JOE: What?

BRAD: Peanut butter! I love peanut butter.

[LIGHTS UP ON LIVING ROOM]

DARLENE: It only makes sense, Joanie. Take what sounds good and believe whatever works for you.

JOAN: There just seems to be something not quite right about that.

DARLENE: Aw, come on, whatever works, right?

[LIGHTS UP ON KITCHEN]

BRAD: I think it's ready, Joe. The peanut butter did the trick.

JOE: I don't know Brad. There's just something not quite right about this. It's not really Chinese food.

BRAD: We'll serve it on china. With the lights really [Looks at food] REALLY dim.

JOE: I guess.

BRAD: Hey, whatever works, right?

[BLACKOUT]

As creative as God encourages us to be, as free as we are to explore our options, combining certain ideas and ingredients can be a recipe for disaster. God's guidelines, His recipe of ingredients if you will, are for us to read and follow for our enjoyment, health benefits, and safety sake. When we don't have all that the recipe in front of us calls for, and we're too proud or stubborn to do what it takes to follow directions, we try substituting anything that might work. And, when peanut butter doesn't do the trick, we tend to blame the recipe and throw it out with the inedible mess we just made.

When something really disappointing or incredibly traumatic happens and you can't believe or understand why God didn't stop it, it's only natural to throw out what suddenly seems like just a notion, that God is loving and good. How could a loving God allow that kind of suffering? Why doesn't He protect innocent children? And so, we try to find a line of reasoning or a belief system that makes more sense to us. We look for something that lines up with our experiences and perspective instead of bringing our perspective gained from experience into alignment with the clarity of God's Word about His character and the truth of His promises.

We know satan's obsession is to destroy God's creation through God's own image-bearers — to shame, accuse, and condemn them day and night — starting the cycle by attacking the most innocent and vulnerable. But isn't it such an "in-your-face" victory for God to say, "Even babies can conquer your attempts and attacks, satan! By the Blood of the Lamb, I can use the mouths of babes to defeat you. My love overrides your evil. My power heals any and every wound you inflict. In fact, My kids will be even mightier and more effective warriors having endured the battle since birth. I, Jehovah Rapha, remove all damage, scars, marks, impurity, rejection, and confusion. "Innocence" is spiritual. I created them innocent to begin with and I will recreate them innocent again, restoring complete wholeness to every fiber of their being. My love casts out ALL fear. You are a defeated foe. You, satan, can NOT impose your likeness on Mine, and because I can heal and restore ANYTHING you mar, to better than new, you have no ammunition left. I have even taken the sting out of death, the power out of trauma, the negative long-term effects out of torment, and can turn around all inflicted pain or suffering to actually benefit My children by gracing them through, strengthening their character, and giving them beauty for ashes."

So where was Jesus in the most traumatic moments of your childhood? He was there with you. But He wasn't just standing there watching or holding your hand. He had thrown Himself between you and your assailant, absorbing the wrath and evil, taking the brunt of the enemy's assault (meant to kill you). He was the One being tortured. He was the One being violated by satan, taking the full fury, crying out, "You can't have this one, devil! This one's Mine!" Any trauma, any harm that came through to you, can and will be reversed, erased, and healed. Jesus took into His own body all eternal consequences. Any temporary pain (for despite how it feels or how long you have suffered, that is what it is, temporary) any fear or torment caused by the human agent used by the devil, Jesus promises to remove it from you forever. Restoration is yours! Freedom is yours! Victory is yours here and now... and forever more!

Jesus bought back our authority to rule the earth, trample on snakes and scorpions, and overcome all the power of the enemy. Nothing can harm us (see Luke 10:19). He has done the hardest part, the impossible, and miraculously given us back the keys to the Kingdom.

What if God's mission for us now is to help reclaim His entire creation from the mess that we, His highest of creatures, created? Like when an adult gets the paper towels, hands them to the child, and instructs them how to wipe up their own careless spill, God has instructed us to go set captives free, raise the dead, cleanse the leper, heal the sick, and preach the Good News that we have access once again to the Kingdom of Heaven. We have access to God our Father through Jesus' Blood. We are equipped and commissioned by the Lord of Angel Armies, Who is fighting by our side, to take back the territory originally meant for us to enjoy. He wants us to fulfill our calling to subdue the earth, to shepherd, nurture, and now to make disciples of the nations using his Kingdom principles and designs. Tell them Jesus is coming back to reign from Jerusalem, and very soon! Spread the Word! The Kingdom of God will be here on earth, literally Heaven on Earth!

We are created to overcome the opposition and prove that even a reflection of God's Glory is stronger, brighter, and more powerful than anything created. He is God and He is Good! Mighty to save! He uses the foolish to confound the wise. We are clueless, but can channel His wisdom. We are weak, but we manifest His power. History shows us, the battle belongs to the Lord! And the Lord ALWAYS wins!

With Blood so pure, so strong, erasing every wrong. So now we can belong to You. Your Love sings us a song and we just sing along. Forever we'll sing on to You... of Ribbons Red.

Chapter 11: The Least We Can Do /WORSHIP

[LIGHTS UP. Steve enters. Joe follows Steve in.]

JOE: But Steve, Steve, you saved my life.

STEVE: I'm glad I was there to help.

JOE: If it wasn't for you I could have been um… you know… CAPUT.

STEVE: Well, you would have done the same for me, right?

JOE: Uh… Is this a trick question?

STEVE: No, Joe. I'm just saying that we're friends and friends take care of each other.

JOE: Yeah, and now I owe you big time.

STEVE: You don't owe me anything.

JOE: You saved my life. I gotta repay you somehow.

STEVE: Forget it, Joe. It was no big deal.

JOE: Steve, if it wasn't for you, I'd be… you know… [Makes slicing motion across throat] I wanna do something to show you how much I… uh… appreciate it.

STEVE: It's really okay. Don't worry about it.

JOE: Look, if you're ever gonna get hit by a car, I'll push you out of the way or something.

STEVE: Thanks, Joe. I'm not expecting to be hit in the near future but...

JOE: Oh, you're right. You might not ever get almost hit. Drat! How am I gonna pay you back?

STEVE: You don't have to pay me back.

JOE: If we were in some other country or something, after saving my life, I'd have to be your servant. I saw it on Gilligan's Island once. The Skipper pulled Gilligan away from the edge of an active volcano... Gilligan was teetering on...

STEVE (Interrupts): Look Joe, I'm just happy you're okay.

JOE: You don't get it, Steve, do you?

STEVE: I guess not. Get what?

JOE: My Gilligan's Island analogy. I'm not gonna leave until you let me do something for you.

STEVE: You're serious.

JOE: Dead serious. [Laughs at himself] Dead serious, get it?

STEVE: Okay, Joe, if it will make you go... (Corrects himself) uh, feel better, I'll think of something.

JOE: Great! Now we're getting somewhere.

STEVE: Hmm... I'd like an ice cream cone about now.

JOE: I don't think so.

STEVE: What?

JOE: Ice cream is bad for you. Too much fat. I'd be helping to clog your arteries. Think of something else.

STEVE: Okay… I'm staining my deck Saturday. You wanna help me?

JOE: I'd love to Steve. But, um… are you using that deck staining stuff?

STEVE: Yeah.

JOE: No can do. Sorry! The fumes give me a headache. Try again.

STEVE: You really don't have to do anything, you know.

JOE: Course I do, Steve. How could I live with myself knowing that you saved my life and I never did anything to pay you back? Think of something, Steve. Come on, have a heart!

STEVE [Sighs]: My car could use a washing.

JOE: Wash your car? That's not good enough. You saved my life. I owe you more than a car wash. Come on, think of something really good. (To audience) Wash his car. Lights on, nobody home.

STEVE (Thinking out loud): A new car would be nice.

JOE: What are you saying here, Steve?

STEVE: Nothing, Joe, just thinking out loud.

JOE: You want I should, ah, buy you a new car?

STEVE: No, of course not. I didn't say that. I just thought…

JOE (Interrupts): That's a great idea!

STEVE: It is?

JOE: A brand new… [Describes dream car]

STEVE: I couldn't ask you to…

JOE: Don't be silly. You saved my life. It's the least I can do.

STEVE: I really could use a new car.

JOE: Then it's settled.

STEVE: But, it really doesn't have to be so elaborate.

JOE: Nothin' but the best for my friend, Steve. Just one thing.

STEVE: What?

JOE: Could you, like maybe, co-sign the loan. I don't exactly have a job right now, and since I declared bankruptcy last month my credit rating isn't exactly flawless.

STEVE: I really don't need a new car, Joe. I just realized the one I have is fine.

JOE: You sure?

STEVE: I'm sure.

JOE: Can't say I didn't try and it's the thought that counts, right?

STEVE: Right.

JOE [Shakes Steve's hand]: Well thanks, Steve, and I forgive you.

STEVE: You forgive me?

JOE: Yeah, for not being able to think of something for me to do to pay you back. I forgive you.

STEVE: Thanks, Joe.

JOE: Remember, if a car is ever gonna hit you, call me. [Exits]

STEVE: I'll do that Joe. Bye.

[BLACKOUT]

What would YOU say? I mean, how would you begin to try to repay someone who actually saved your life? Would you even let yourself think about what your life (or lack of it) would have been like if they hadn't stepped in? Okay, so maybe we don't have a lot of everyday experience with super heroes rescuing us from certain peril, but most of us can at least relate to someone taking the blame or covering up a mistake for us. Maybe a good friend pointed something out that would have otherwise caused you embarrassment: a piece of spinach stuck smack on the middle of your front tooth just before your interview; or maybe two different shoes on your feet just before you left for the wedding, because you were trying to decide which looked better and then got distracted. Maybe somebody rescued you with, "No, let me tell you what that word REALLY means before you use it during your big presentation." There would be many "thank yous" to be sure. Being spared humiliation leaves you grateful. But what about when your very life has been spared, especially when someone else's suffering has eased yours?

Some of you may have been rescued from a fire or an accident by a brave public servant or even a heroic stranger, so you know first-hand how you'd respond. But most of us haven't been in that kind of peril. We've only experienced it vicariously through suspenseful action films or stories when one of the main characters is trapped by the villain and the hero has to save them at the risk of their own life. And yet as predictable as the rescue is, we get inspired by the hero's courage, while empathizing with the gratitude, love, and relief of the rescued one. Maybe that's because it mirrors so closely our own story, the one written in our hearts by the Rescuer Himself.

You see, at just the right time, when we were still powerless, Christ died for the ungodly. Very rarely will anyone die for a righteous man, though for a good man someone might possibly dare to die. But God demonstrates His own Love for us in this: While we were still sinners, Christ died for us. He was delivered over to death for our sins and was raised to life for our justification. By His stripes we are healed (see Romans 5:6-8 and Isaiah 4:25).

We didn't ask for His help. We weren't even born yet, but Jesus made a way for us to be rescued. But rescued from what? Maybe you feel like you've got this "life thing" under control. No rescue necessary. You think that Jesus dying on the cross to prove His love, and to show us how to stand up for what we believe in, and to be willing to die for good causes was really noble and all, so thanks for the great example there, God. But honestly, it was kind of extreme don't you think? Too bad nothing really came of it.

So maybe you do have life under control, but what about the "death thing" or the "life after death thing"? Truth is, Jesus dying on the cross would only make sense if we would somehow be in great danger if He hadn't. It would be insane for Jesus to lay down His life, be tortured and crucified for us, if we didn't need to be rescued from something really big and very bad.

God's Word tells us in Romans 6:23, "the wages of sin is death, but the gift of God is eternal life in Christ Jesus our Lord." If the gift of eternal life in Christ Jesus seems too unnatural, and life after death doesn't really make sense to you, maybe you've convinced yourself that death isn't really such a bad thing because all it means is that you'll cease to exist. You see it as just a natural part of life and really no big deal. Okay, then tell me again, why do we try to avoid it? Why does it feel so wrong to us and so painful when someone dies, like it's going against the grain of how our spirit is telling us things should be? If death isn't such a big deal, why was it the consequence God warned Adam and Eve about if they ate from the Tree of the Knowledge of Good and Evil? Even if it's just a story for you, why is death so threatening?

To eat from that tree meant that they desired something more than they already had. They wanted to be like God, but the truth is they were already created in His image. They had His goodness, His innocence. What they lacked living in innocence was the knowledge of evil, and the knowledge of what STRIVING to be good was like. They had the option to remain innocent, living forever, content in God's Kingdom with access to His wisdom. Or they could question God's character and trust in satan's twisted truth that eating from the forbidden tree would give them knowledge equal to God's.

We find ourselves here and now with a similar option: to question God's character and trust in satan's twisted truth, or to accept Jesus' offer to restore our innocence, resurrect our spirits, and give us access once again to God's wisdom. Jesus holds out His gift of grace and life to us, and we toss it aside thinking we're better off without God hovering over us, telling us what to do all the time. But independence means "not connected, unsupported, to be separated from." To be separated from God, to be independent of Him, sounds more like an accurate definition of death, rather than freedom.

Every death, every loss we experience, every tear shed at a farewell service, is a reminder of God's heartache over the choice mankind made to live independently of Him. When Jesus wept at the tomb of Lazarus, He was experiencing the double grief of losing a friend to death as a Man, and losing mankind to death as a Friend. This overwhelming grief Jesus felt, just weeks before the Cross, I believe, solidified His resolve and drove Him forward to absorb death (the wages of our sin) into His innocent body. He knew that shedding His sinless Blood was the only way to revive the spirits of His lost friends, His Father's children, His Promised Bride to Be — His Church.

If there was any other avenue for us to be reconciled to Father God, any other way for our spirits to be resurrected and connected back to communion life with our Creator, don't you think God would have thought of it, especially when Jesus pleaded, "If there's any other way, let this cup pass from Me"? The risk our Loving Father took creating us with a free will so we could choose to be rescued from death or not, costs Him, over and over, the Heartache of heartaches: rejection by His own children, knowing that their choice of independence means eternal separation.

Suppose you decided to persevere through a horrible second job putting in long ghastly hours of painfully exhausting labor, to earn the money it would take to get your loved one out of overwhelming debt (a debt so big they could never do it themselves). You were willing to suffer to see them free from the slavery of it, once again able to breathe and enjoy life. Then after years of sacrifice, you were finally able to present them with the ransom money you slaved for. Imagine if they said, "Aw, how nice of you, but that's okay. I got myself into this mess. I'll get myself out. I really wish you hadn't done that though. You're kind of making me feel bad, like you don't think I'm capable or something. I'll have you know I keep up just fine with my minimum monthly payments… for the most part. So thanks, but no thanks. You can keep it. I have my pride, ya know." Can you imagine?

We all have our pride, yes we know. Well, except for you, right? You're pretty humble, I bet. So let me ask you this: Have you not taken money or advantage of a favor from someone before because you didn't want to owe them? Or are you embarrassed by your obvious need for assistance? "No thanks, I got this." Have someone's hurtful words, "you're worthless," or "you'll never make it on your own," sent you on an all-consuming life's mission to prove them wrong, no matter what? Whatever it is that makes it hard for you to admit you need rescuing, God's love is bigger and He will lovingly pursue you, till the day you die.

The resurrection power to resuscitate your spirit was only realized by Jesus' absolute humility. He surrendered Himself to naked humiliation and torture so that we'd have an option to be spiritually clothed in His righteousness and covered and protected by His Blood. He humbled Himself to death to give us life. Wouldn't it stand to reason that it takes humility like the faith of a child to say, "Jesus, save me"? Even if you didn't ask to be rescued, or maybe you've been too proud or embarrassed up to this point, Jesus' offer of abundant life in communion with your Maker from here on out still stands. But there is a deadline to humbly accept it, and you never know when your personal deadline will be. Now back to our original question: How would you try to repay someone who actually saved your life?

I know I dated myself at the beginning of this chapter by referencing "Gilligan's Island" in the sketch, but the idea of becoming someone's servant for life was not just thought up for that old TV sitcom. Our natural response is to somehow try and repay our debt, and a life of service for a life saved makes sense to us.

Suddenly, if all your financial debt was miraculously paid off by someone, completely forgiven, and you only had to work for the fun of it, wouldn't you at least want to write that someone a thank you note? Jesus wants to deposit into our spiritual accounts everything we'll ever need to live spiritually free from debt forever. All we have to do is admit our need to be rescued and humbly accept His gift. Then we can just work for the fun of it in His Kingdom. But what does serving Jesus, just working for fun, look like? How do you do it day to day?

In a way, using your gifts, resources and talents to edify, serve, and bless those around you (especially "the least of these" as Jesus said) is like blessing Jesus Himself — a life of service for saving your life.

When you realize the fact that being saved by Jesus is for all eternity, it would probably prompt you to want to pay tribute to Him publicly. You'd sing His praises to everybody you meet, and you'd sing praises TO Him, with others whom He also rescued. You'd tell each other what He's done for you and how much He means to you. Hmm, sounds kinda like worship, doesn't it?

"Just Sing His Name"

With trembling lips we whisper. In reverent fear we cry. Your Glory leaves us speechless. All we can do is try and find our voice to thank You, but silently we bow. All poetry and music seem inadequate somehow.

What do you sing for a King? What do you say to the Judge who forgave you; the Brother who saved you; the Father who made you? What gift could you possibly bring the Creator of everything?

Our lips are so unholy. Our minds can't understand. You call us Your Beloved and reach to us Your Hand, "Come sing for Me, My Dear Ones, just for a little while. To see you dance and clap for Me, it makes a Father smile. I know you're not yet perfect. I love you just the same. I wish you knew the joy you bring each time you sing My Name. Come sing My Name."

What do you sing for a King? What do you say to the Judge who forgave you; the Brother who saved you; the Father who made you? What gift could you possibly bring the Creator of everything? Just sing His Name!

Your Majesty, Your Honor, Our Savior, Father God, with gratefulness, Lord Jesus, we dance and applaud and sing Your Name.

What do you sing for a King? ...Just sing His Name.

Chapter 12: Whatever Happened to Happily

Ever After? /LOSS

When our daughter was new at talking, and listening to her renditions of the Alphabet Song, among a few others, was part of our family's entertainment, my sister taught her a phrase that started to become as entertaining as her songs — "I lost the mood." Little 18-month-old Kimmy would sing, "A B C D E F G H I... I loss da moot," and we'd all laugh and clap. But loss for most of us is usually not such a laughing matter, and it begins for all of us at birth.

With our very first breath of life, each of us experiences loss — loss of our cushioned, safe and cozy nest, and loss of the most unique connection to another human life we'll ever have. I wonder if THAT'S why babies cry. But with that necessary loss, we gained more than just a belly button. We gained a new way of life, new breath, and a brand-new beginning in a whole new world.

Most of us don't record accounts of this dramatic loss in our memoirs (seeing as our memories of it are probably a bit fuzzy to say the least), but we may recall instead another necessary loss as being our first. It's a loss made only tolerable by excited parents, a shiny new quarter (or with inflation maybe a dollar) under our pillow, in exchange for what was once an intricate part of our smile. And with it came the promise of a new, bigger, better permanent one to take its place. All

159

that gained, to make up for that one loss. It was still hard, but it softened the blow.

Trying to find anything positive associated with loss is pretty challenging for me. The very word "loss" sounds sad and defeated, doesn't it? Unless it's preceded by "weight," then it just makes me feel guilty, but it's the one time, for most of us, that it actually sounds good.

As much as I like Joni Mitchell's catchy tune and clever lyrics, "Don't it always seem to go that you don't know whatcha got till it's gone…" the process of feeling, grieving, and accepting loss has got to be one of the most exhausting and perspective changing there is.

Sometimes it's purely a matter of our perspective that makes a "loss" a loss. The loss is actually love. Let me explain. Parents, caregivers, and pet owners can all tell you the response they'll get when they need to take away and put out of reach an item or object that could cause harm to their charges. But all the whining, crying, and barking will not sway the caregiver to give in because… they care! They can see the potential danger and they are doing the loving thing by withholding the desired object. What feels like loss is actually love. It still hurts like loss, but to get it back could cause even more pain.

Since God never wastes suffering, there just has to be some sort of lesson with all the pain that accompanies loss, some kind of benefit in all of it, wouldn't you think? But what? It just hurts. We suffer loss and we ask God, "Do You understand how much this hurts? Do You even get it?"

Oh yeah, He gets it! We grieve loss BECAUSE we're made in God's likeness. God grieved that He made mankind when He saw how far we had fallen from His presence and His likeness, how much we had lost, and how miserable we had become. Our Creator not only suffered His loss of us, but He compassionately suffered along with us, our loss of the capacity to fully know Him. As an act of kindness, He destroyed His once perfect creation and all He dearly loved before it suffered any more of its painfully slow self-destruction. Darkness had violated and defiled God's image-bearers making the Nephilim outnumber the pure. Nephilim were half human, half demonic creatures often written about in mythology, but Scripture and archeological evidence tells us they actually existed. Noah and his family were all who were left undefiled by demonic influence. And Noah grieved with God as God's mercy flooded the earth.

If you've ever had a basement flood, you understand the loss caused by water damage. If you've suffered through a cataclysmic flood or fire and lost everything you owned, you understand drastic life-altering loss. But if your loved one was lost in that disaster… that's a devastating loss that just can't be understood.

I have to believe our perfect Heavenly Father understands the pain and grief of devastating loss more than any of us ever will. The loss God feels when one of His kids chooses to leave home forever and not come back, to live forever independently of Him, must devastate Him beyond our human experience. It's this tragic loss that Father God suffers with each final goodbye, knowing that this is the risk He took leaving the choice up to us. The pain of loss drove Him to the drastic measure of the Cross. It was the risk He was willing to die for so we could have our free will to choose Him. Such perfect love!

If we as imperfect parents know how to soften the blow of loss for our children, how much more will our empathetic Heavenly Daddy give the gift of the Holy Spirit (The Comforter) to those who suffer loss, to all who ask (see Luke 11:13)? No matter the cause or depth of our loss, Holy Spirit understands, especially when we just can't wrap our heads around it. The shock of loss leaves us dazed. He's there to give us peace beyond understanding, when nothing else makes sense.

The death of a loved one, I think you'll agree, is the ultimate loss. But the unforeseen "death" of a relationship, without any reason or forewarning, has to be the most baffling and taunting of losses for me. No conflict, no blowups, just unreturned calls or texts, with no explanation. Now I know what you're thinking, "What did you do? What didn't you do? You must be a real winner to lose friends like that." Those are all my thoughts too. If you've suffered through that kind of loss, now you know you're not alone. There's at least one other person, and here I am. But here's what I think: I'm beginning to see, and I'm learning it from the seasons, that with the passing of one, comes the newness of another. Unlike a new tooth, a season isn't necessarily bigger, better, or permanent. But it is new and different and purposeful, and it happens without any word or assistance from me. Like it or not, it happens. My whole world changes around me. I didn't cause it and it's not my fault. It just changed, despite me.

I'm starting to understand that God is directing seasons of my life because I asked Him to. And like a great stage manager, Holy Spirit sees to it that every detail and prop is in place and the actors are cued for their scene so it can go without a hitch (now if I can just remember my lines).

There are going to be certain scenes in our lives that are written and set for certain characters. If someone from the wrong scene mistakenly wandered onto the stage, it could really make things awkward. Imagine if a character whose final goodbye scene with you at the end of Act I (putting a really interesting twist in the storyline) were to suddenly show back up in Act II because the actor missed being on stage with you. As sentimental as you might feel, the Director would probably not share the same sentiment. When it's a new scene, a change of season, there will be other characters to keep the story flowing. If a line is dropped or a cue missed, there will be other players to adlib with and get back on script with.

But what about when an integral character in your scene doesn't make an entrance? Someone you were counting on, no fault of their own, has had a costume malfunction and they're desperately trying to free themselves, but there you are suddenly left on stage, alone, in the spotlight, with what seems like a million eyes staring at you. You're at a total loss for words. You know this scene is pivotal to the plot and your fellow cast member is the only one who can deliver the lines needed, but there you are… alone. You hear the Director in a stage whisper say, "You can do this. Just keep talking." And then when you're about to crawl under the giant papier-mâché prop of a rock, you hear the Prompter from offstage, as if from behind a tree, saying the lines that set up your dialogue and effectively move the story along.

And you realize, "I'm not alone. I may be the only one on stage, but I'm not alone."

Don't listen to the hecklers trying to make you feel rejected or abandoned. Sometimes it's just a costume malfunction. Sometimes the script calls for new characters to enter and others to exit. Just trust in God's experience and vision, take direction well, and enjoy the story you're helping make happen. Remember that the Director hand-picked you for this part and He knows you can do it. He believes in you.

I guess I've been thinking about the "lessons of loss" for a while now, because in 2009 I wrote a Christmas production called "Twinkle" that addressed it, and I didn't realize it until now. I'd like to share the last two scenes with you, but let me set the stage with some of the intro and brief overview I wrote for the cast:

> There is a dimension hidden in our souls that serves as a witness to the reality of more than our senses can perceive. It speaks to us like a twinkle in someone's eye, letting us in on what is about to happen. Like stars that tell stories and reveal a realm beyond our immediate reach, the Morning Star, Messiah, slipped into our three-dimensional world and brought with Him amazing possibilities. He spoke of the realm of faith and believing without seeing, but not without proof. Jesus is the Proof. And for those of us who need something visible here and now, we need to do nothing more but look up to the night sky and see the evidence twinkle before us…

Each scene begins with a few lines spoken before the lights come up. It's played with just one modern-day setting: the backyard of a house, with a picnic table and the main focus, a tire swing. The huge tree it hangs from is imagined offstage right. A small pine tree near the house, stage left, grows scene by scene to depict the passage of time.

The main characters, Tyler Jones and Stephanie (the girl next door) are portrayed at three stages of their life: Junior High School, then in their twenties, and finally as 50-yr.-olds in Act II. Some lines are actually read offstage by the younger versions of their characters as Tyler remembers past events.

I've started you off with the opening song lyrics, "Close Your Eyes," which is sung in the dark as a spotlight shines on the swing. The scenes that follow are from Act II. Tyler, now 50 years old, is married to his childhood sweetheart, Stephanie. They have a grown daughter, Taylor, and live in the same house Tyler grew up in. Because their names are so similar to read, I've listed Tyler (the dad) as T.J. to be less confusing.

Act II, Scene 1, is set at night, as every scene before it has been, from December to December. And though you haven't seen any of the rest of it, I hope you can now enjoy the conclusion of "Twinkle." Blackout. Spotlight on the tire swing. Cue Music:

"Close Your Eyes"

Close your eyes and hold on tight. Take it in like Christmas night.
Light a candle, sing a song. Twinkle, twinkle, sing along.

Close your eyes and touch the sky. 'Member when it made you cry.
Take a leap, land on a cloud. Hear the wind and laugh out loud.

Twinkle, and your heart is there, whispering a hopeful prayer,
Dangling without a care, trusting God is everywhere.

Close your eyes and open wide. Take a taste and be surprised.
Go ahead spin it around. Pick your feet up off the ground.

If you really want to see what life is meant to be,
Stop list'ning to the voice of reason. Like children from the start,
Start seeing with your heart and make your life a Christmas season.

"Twinkle" ACT II Scene 1

[WITH LIGHTS OUT]

T.J.: Aren't they beautiful? …Taylor.

TAYLOR (Grumpy): It's cold out here.

T.J.: I know, but aren't they beautiful? Just look at 'em.

TAYLOR: What, the stars?

[LIGHTS UP]

T.J. (Bah): The stars! You sound like your mother. No, these [Holds up tickets]. The two most beautiful tickets of a Christmas present I've seen in a long time: Celtics vs. Lakers, front row center court, the TD Garden. Doesn't get any better. I'm glad she gave it to us early so now we can come up with a really great gift for her! She thinks we're out here fixing the lights, but I really wanted to talk to you about what to get her. Any ideas?

TAYLOR: You don't have to keep up the act, Dad. I know.

T.J.: What act? I'm excited and you should be too. TWO tickets, me and you! KG, Paul Pierce, Rajon Rondo… He's the one you think is cute, right?

TAYLOR: No, I just think he's a great player.

T.J.: Oh, right, of course, a great player. (Sarcastically) Uh huh.

TAYLOR: Really, Dad. Cut it out. Mom told me.

T.J.: Told you what?

TAYLOR: Only the most devastating news a grown child could hear before Christmas time.

T.J.: She told you? Already? We were trying to spare you as long as we could.

TAYLOR: How long have you known?

T.J.: We saw the lawyer last week. We tried everything. There's nothing else we can do. It's just inevitable.

TAYLOR: But you need to fight for this! You guys have such memories. You've told me all the stories – that first Christmas, your leap of faith, your first kiss. Years of history about to be chopped up and pulverized! Don't you wanna just pulverize him for doing this?

T.J.: I did at first, but then I realized it's not his fault. It's like a disease or something. It gets inside and makes everything weaker and weaker. This is the best thing to do, Honey. And he's paying for it, believe me.

TAYLOR: I'll make him pay for it all right.

T.J.: Taylor!

TAYLOR: How can you guys be so cool with this? This is like up there with "You shall not murder." I mean why does it hafta happen?

T.J.: The expert said…

TAYLOR: What expert? I want another opinion.

T.J.: Even if the expert is wrong. Even if it is perfectly healthy…

TAYLOR: Which it is!

T.J.: It's not our tree, Taylor.

TAYLOR: But your names are on it – you and Mom's. "Steph and Tyler 4eva" with a heart. And the swing. What about the swing? More than seven years. Eminent domain!

T.J.: But the tree is not on our property. Look at the marker. Gram and Gramps let Papa hang the swing 'cause Mom and I were such good friends. And when we got married and moved in to Nana and Papa's house it was kind of like it was our tree for a while, but with Gram and Gramps gone now, legally it's not ours. It's Sam's.

TAYLOR: I'll just go have a little talk with him.

T.J.: We already did, and with our lawyer. He has every right to cut it down. Even if it's not diseased.

TAYLOR: But what about New Year's Eve? How are we gonna do our traditional "Swinging in the New Year?"

T.J.: We'll hafta find another branch to put the swing on.

TAYLOR: There IS no other branch. You said so yourself. Your dad said so. This is the perfect branch. As strong and thick as most trunks. Nothing else could hold us up like this branch.

T.J.: It is a great tree. And it does look perfectly healthy.

TAYLOR: You know it is. He just wants more sun in his yard.

T.J.: We'll have less leaves to rake?

TAYLOR: How can you say that? It's our tree we're talking about.

T.J.: It's not our tree.

TAYLOR: Well, it's not his either. He didn't plant it.

T.J.: Neither did we. Whose tree is it really?

TAYLOR: Mine?

T.J.: Who made the tree?

TAYLOR (Resigns): I know. It's God's tree. But He gave it to me.

T.J.: To enjoy for a season. And God only knows, maybe the tree is diseased. It could fall on the house the next blizzard or ice storm.

TAYLOR: God wouldn't let that happen.

T.J.: Which may be exactly why Sam is having it cut down Saturday.

TAYLOR: Saturday! This Saturday?

T.J.: Mom didn't tell you that part, huh?

TAYLOR: Daddy, do something! You gotta fix it somehow. Don't let him take the tree down.

T.J.: What would you have me do? Chain myself to it?

TAYLOR: Would that work?

T.J.: I don't think so.

TAYLOR: Maybe you AND Mom, together?

T.J.: I think the best thing we can do is enjoy it while we still have it. You wanna swing?

TAYLOR: I can't even look at it without crying. Besides, it's diseased, remember? The branch will probably break. [Runs inside]

T.J.: [Walks to swing, looks up at tree] We go back a long way, don't we. You've been more faithful then most friends. Can't believe I'm gonna hafta say goodbye to you. You've held me up this far, diseased or not, let's ride! [Gets on swing] Oh yeah, right back. There's the creak of your branch. Like music.

["Break of Day" music begins in the background, then memory voices of young adult Steph and Tyler are spoken into mikes from offstage.]

STEPH: *Star light, star bright, first star I see tonight, I wish I may, I wish I might, have this wish I wish tonight.*

TY: *Uh, Steph, aren't you a little old for that?*

STEPH: *You're a 22-year-old man being pushed on a tire swing and you're telling me I'm too old to make a wish?*

TY: *Whaddya wish for?*

STEPH: *Can't tell ya, Ty, or it won't come true.*

TY: *Has one ever come true?*

STEPH: *Yeah... you're still my best friend.*

[Pause indicating passage of time]

STEPH: *Oh, Tyler. It's beautiful, look how it twinkles.*

TY: *You mean sparkles.*

STEPH: *No, this diamond twinkles like the stars in the sky.*

TY: *Well, do you want to keep it then?*

STEPH: *Do I have to marry you to keep it?*

TY: *Absolutely.*

STEPH: *Then, yes, I wanna keep it.*

TY: *Okay. My turn on the swing.*

STEPH: *How bout I just move over.*

[Pause indicating passage of time]

STEPH (Calls): *Tyler? Oh, there you are! Testing the new rope?*

TY: *I have to make sure it's safe, ya know, for the neighborhood kids and all.*

STEPH: *Well, they're gonna hafta learn to share it.*

TY: *Oh, they let me have a turn once and a while.*

STEPH: *No, I meant they'll have to learn to share it with your new daughter.*

TY: *It's a girl?*

STEPH: *I've got a picture. Look, isn't she beautiful?*

TY: *Beautiful. Um… where is she?*

STEPH: *I'm not sure. Maybe that blob right there. But the ultrasound technician assures me it's a beautiful girl.*

TY: *Beautiful.*

[Music stops]

T.J.: [Looks up at tree] Beautiful. Thanks, old friend. Thanks for helping me hold on.

STEPHANIE (Calls from offstage): Tyler?

T.J.: Stephanie?

STEPHANIE: Supper!

T.J.: I'm coming. [Gets off the swing] Do I smell cookies?

STEPHANIE: Your Mom's famous recipe. I saved you some dough.

T.J.: You're a good friend! [Exits into house]

[BLACKOUT]

"Break of Day"

I don't wanna say goodbye. I don't want our time to end.
Like the stars up in the sky, I could count on you my friend,
To be there in my night, to comfort me with light
until I see the break of day.

I hold every memory, each hello and sad goodbye,
Like the branches of a tree hold each leaf up to the sky,
Basking in the One who sends both rain and Sun,
To grow us stronger day by day.

God knows goodbye can break a heart.
Each time we turn and walk away He feels the pain that's tearing
us apart, and like a gentle rain He whispers, "Hey…

…I will never say goodbye. I'll forever be your Friend.
If the stars fade in the sky, still My Love for you won't end.
I'm there in your night to comfort you with Light
until you see the break of day."

God allows the pain, like a pelting rain,
to wake us back to life again.

ACT II Scene 2 ~ That following Saturday, midafternoon.

[WITH NO LIGHT]

BILLY: Isn't she beautiful?

T.J.: More than beautiful. How old do you think 150, 200 years?

[LIGHTS UP]

BILLY [Holding up chainsaw]: Whaddya talkin'? I just got her two days ago. Early Christmas present from the wife. Haven't tried her yet, but she'll make mulch out of any tree in her path in half the time. So where's the sick tree? Let's get to work.

T.J.: You don't know which one? But aren't you the expert that told Sam his tree was diseased?

BILLY: No, he called and told ME he had a sick tree. A BIG sick tree, so I decided I needed to get me a big sick chainsaw. The one I had just wasn't… BIG enough. I worked it out with my wife that this would be my early Christmas present, and birthday, and anniversary. Isn't she beautiful?

T.J.: That was very nice of her.

BILLY: No, not Phyllis, this. [The chainsaw]

T.J. (Trying to stall): She's a beaute, alright. Look at that shiny chrome. Too bad it will never look as beautiful after today. Maybe we should take a picture. I'll go get my camera.

BILLY: No, this baby looks even better covered in sawdust and sap. So let's feed her, huh? Where's the sick tree?

T.J.: Shouldn't we wait for Sam?

BILLY: Oh, no, he's away. He prepaid and left town for the holidays. I do believe that's how Phyllis got me this new chainsaw. So I best use it, as to not disappoint my paying customer. He said if I had any questions, I could ask you.

T.J.: So Sam didn't know you were a tree EXPERT, he just thought you cut them down?

BILLY: Well, I don't like to toot my own horn. Pride goes before a fall.

T.J.: So they say.

BILLY: So they say "Timber!" …So they say before a fall, get it?

T.J.: I get it.

BILLY: I got a million of 'em.

T.J.: You're a real "cut up," huh?

BILLY: Hey, good one. But I "saw" it comin'. [Laughs at himself, then clears his throat] Well, I better get to work before it gets too dark. Can't really cut a tree down in the dark now, can you. So which tree is it?

T.J.: Would you like something cold to drink first?

BILLY: No thanks, I really need to…

T.J.: Christmas cookies?

BILLY: No, we're losing light here.

T.J.: How 'bout some nice hot cocoa. It'll just take a minute.

BILLY: If I didn't know better, I'd think you were stalling or something.

T.J.: Just trying to be hospitable.

BILLY: Then could you please be hospitable enough to tell me which tree is coming down today?

T.J.: I thought you could tell just by looking at them.

BILLY: I can. I'm gifted that way. That's what has me baffled. Your neighbor said it was in the corner of his yard. This is the only tree I see in the corner, but he can't mean this one. This is a beauty. Great tire swing. Besides, this is on your property.

T.J.: As much as it kills me to say this, this is the tree Sam wants cut down.

BILLY: Why would you wanna have this tree cut down? It's like the granddaddy of all trees. And it's perfectly healthy.

T.J.: I KNEW it. Maybe he thinks it has too many leaves or something?

BILLY: Well, how'd you get Sam to pay for it, being your tree and all? And why did you have him tell me it was sick?

T.J.: I didn't tell him it was sick, and it's not my tree!

BILLY: It's on your property.

T.J.: No, it's not. My property ends where the marker is.

BILLY: Begging your pardon, Mr. um...

T.J.: Tyler, call me, Tyler.

BILLY: Mr. Tyler, I do my research as to not cut down someone else's tree by mistake. That can cause a lot of trouble, believe me. I thought that woman would never stop yelling. Oh, how she went on. I didn't know a human voice could reach that pitch. Almost to the dog whistle stage, but still audible. Anyhow, live and learn. That's my new motto.

T.J.: So what about the property line?

BILLY: Well you see, that was the problem. I never checked that lady's property line, hence my new motto. Oh wait, you mean this property line. Of course you do. No, now this I'm sure of. Your property line runs from that tree down there straight to a foot over that side of this granddaddy tree and then over that way. Its huge roots must have displaced the marker to over here, 'stead of over there where it started. Yes sir. This tree is ALL yours.

T.J. (Slowly): I could kiss you!

BILLY (Nervously): A handshake will be just fine.

T.J.: [Shakes his hand vigorously and continuously] You don't know what this means to me. This is an answer to prayer. Thank you! Thank you so much for living, and learning, and doing your research!

BILLY: [Lets go of hand] Maybe the kiss would have been less painful.

T.J.: I can't wait to tell Stephanie and Taylor. My wife and daughter.

BILLY: You have a daughter named Taylor Tyler?

T.J.: No, my FIRST name is Tyler.

BILLY: Tyler Tyler?

T.J.: No. Our last name is Jones.

BILLY: But you said to call you Mr. Tyler?

T.J.: You can call me anything you want. You just gave me the best Christmas present ever! [Moving toward house] I need to let my family know. I better go call or they'll kill me. They went to the movies because they couldn't bear to watch, or even hear, the tree coming down. And now OUR tree, which is perfectly healthy, is NOT coming down. Do you wanna come in and have some cookies NOW?

BILLY: Thanks, but you know what I'd really like? [Whispers something]

T.J.: Of course! As long as you like. [Exits into house]

BILLY: Oh boy! Just like the one near the swimming hole back home. [Jumps on swing] Oh, this is wonderful! If I close my eyes, I can almost hear Mama's voice (Cranky) "William Robert! Get yourself off that thing and do your homework!" I'll get off when I'm good and ready, Mama!

PHYLLIS: [Enters] William Robert! What are you doing?

BILLY: [With eyes closed] It's amazing how much my mama's memory voice sounds like Phyllis'.

PHYLLIS: Maybe because you usually marry someone who reminds you of your mother.

BILLY: That was no memory voice. [Opens eyes] Hello, Phyllis.

PHYLLIS: Is this how you earn a living? Hard work you have there.

BILLY: What are you doing here?

PHYLLIS: You forgot your safety goggles.

BILLY [Feels top of head]: So I did. Well, thanks, but I didn't really need 'em.

PHYLLIS: I can see that.

BILLY: Turns out the tree our customer wanted felled isn't his tree. This great big granddaddy tree here… it's Mr. Tyler's.

PHYLLIS: Sooo… you haven't used your Christmas present yet?

BILLY: I'm sorry, Phyllis. It's not that I don't LOVE it. I do. I just haven't had a chance.

PHYLLIS: Well good. Cause it's going back.

BILLY: What? But it's my best Christmas present ever.

PHYLLIS: Have you forgotten how I paid for this chainsaw?

BILLY: Oh… yes I had. Oh, the irony. What brings one man and his family such great joy and peace, pries the pleasure out of another's Christmas.

PHYLLIS: Since when did you become a philosopher?

BILLY: It's this swing, Phylly. We gotta get us one of these.

PHYLLIS: You do look kinda tranquil up there.

BILLY: You wanna try?

PHYLLIS: No, thank you. Somebody's gotta keep their feet on the ground. Now Billy come on. Why don't you get down and help me take this back to the store. Then we can pay the guy back.

BILLY: [Gets off swing] It was fun while it lasted. But Phyllis, if we bring this back, can we afford to get me a little something else for Christmas?

PHYLLIS: How 'bout some rope? [Exits]

BILLY (As exiting): And I'll give you an old tire. Perfect! [Exits]

[**STAGE LIGHTS FADE. SPOTLIGHT** on swing. Then from offstage, spoken into mikes, the Junior High voices of Steffi and Tyler are heard.]

STEFFI: I'll be right there, Mommy. Tyler?

TYLER: Yeah?

STEFFI: This is a great swing.

TYLER: Yeah, it is.

STEFFI: Aren't you glad we both stopped "being polite" and finally jumped on?

TYLER: Yeah.

STEFFI: Tyler?

TYLER: Yes, Steffi?

STEFFI: Do you think we'll always be friends?

TYLER: Yeah. Do you?

STEFFI: Yeah, I do too. Oh, I better go. My mom called me. Merry Christmas, Tyler!

TYLER: Yeah, okay, you too, Merry Christmas!

[FADE TO BLACK]

God invented happily ever after. It's the only kind of story I can read or movie I can watch without being negatively affected for days. Maybe it's just the side-effects of empathy and a vivid imagination, but for me not to be disturbed by a movie, it has to meet my "Bluebirds of Happiness" criteria:

The heroes have to live. Only characters in the first scene that you hardly know or care about can die (and even then, I'd rather not see it. Just let characters casually mention it in unemotional dialogue).

Love must triumph!

Oh yeah, and *it has to be very funny.*

Not too much suspense. Maybe a tad bit of romantic tension. The more predictable the better.

Beautiful scenery is definitely a plus.

Breaking into musical numbers helps me remember it's just a story (I like musicals).

As you can probably conclude, there aren't many movies out there that I can feel good about. Maybe "Mary Poppins," but even then, when Jane and Michael run away from the bank scene, it's kind of scary. Am I right? Alright, I might be exaggerating a little, but have you noticed how many movies and stories revolve around loss or the threat of loss?

Loss causes conflict that needs resolving. It's a perfect setup for a fund-raising, show-stopping musical production, which highlights the actor's hidden talent (or lack of it) and saves the farm or old homestead from impending foreclosure. It creates the need for a hero to save the day!

But the loss of a main character that you've started to care about and gotten to know? That's just not fair. It may make it closer to real life, but it's supposed to be entertaining me and getting my mind OFF of reality. I've enough reality in my, well... real life.

There was a season for me, not long ago, when we had to leave our church family of 27 years to pursue the call of God's Spirit to use the gifts He had given us, gifts that made the fellow-leaders we loved and served with uneasy. It felt like the closest thing to what I imagine divorce feels like.

A little over a year later, we moved out of our house of 35 years where we had married, raised our family, and renovated three times. We moved to a different state, reluctantly placing my parents in a nursing home. Five months later we said goodbye to my dad, five months after that my mom passed away. Three days later, John Paul Jackson, a well-known prophet I admired and respected, died. Mixed in with all that, and maybe not in this exact order (it was all just a blur) one of our indoor cats had gotten out and started living in the woods. His two-year-old brother died suddenly and inexplicably months after my mom's death. The kitten we had gotten to replace the woods cat had a rare disease and died just before Christmas. And then, three baby chicks of the ten that hatched didn't make it.

Okay, I know cats and chicks and a famous prophet might not seem like such traumatic losses to you, but it was overwhelming. My emotional processor was on overload. It might have been a little more tolerable spread out over time, but after losing both parents five months apart in the middle of such a transitional time of our lives, and baby chicks not making it becomes a big deal. It was all within what seemed like minutes of each other.

I know others who have had similar losses all at once, all in a row. Maybe there's a limit to the depths you can grieve, so you might as well grieve it all at once and get it over with. But either way, with significant loss comes significant lessons that together can change your life and your perspective.

One life-changing lesson in loss was learned watching my dad peacefully exiting this realm. For that brief time, I felt like I had an understanding of something that, up to that point, had felt so mysterious. It was as if my dad was teaching my sister and me, as we sat bedside, "See, this is how you do it." What I saw was just how similar exiting and entering this world really are — the labor and then the delivery from one realm into the other.

When someone we dearly love (who knows Jesus) leaves this nest and is rebirthed into the complete clarity of Heaven, our loss means for them a new way of life, new breath, and a brand new beginning in a whole new world — not starting all over again, but continuing on, this time without loss or limitations.

For a while it all felt very real and affirming, like I just knew that everything I believed about life continuing on into eternity was true. I felt like I had seen my dad cross into Glory. But just like Moses, coming down off the mountain, experienced the fading away of the visible Glory from his face... the cat ran away and then it was Christmas.

Our first Christmas in our new house was also the first Christmas without my dad here. My mom was sick with an infection in a nursing home that was not properly caring for her. Christmas was my mom's holiday. Her love language was giving presents. This was also the first Christmas I was not able to be at my childhood home, my mom's childhood home, the one my grandfather built. Even though my parents lived with us for seven years, my daughter and her husband bought my parent's house, so I had experienced every Christmas of my life there.

Christmas is all about tradition. And all of the traditional places for the decorations to hang were all... missing! They were all back home, in another house, in another state, along with any tidings of comfort and joy to be had. We prayed, held on, and cried our way into the New Year.

Then Valentine's Day night, early Sunday morning, my mom left to be with Jesus, and to see her Valentine (of almost 60 years) again. My long goodbye to a mom who had prayed me through life and become such a good friend had started 11 years before that Valentine's night.

With Alzheimer's, there is loss by loss, year by year, and then day by day. Four years into it, I wrote this song for a character in a play to sing to his grandmother, but it was really a song from my heart to my mom:

"In Time"

I heard your stories; I was listening all along. I didn't show it, but your influence was strong. And even though I yawned, pretending to be smart, the time you spent spoke volumes to my heart.

You didn't know it, but everything you said, the gentle whispers when tucking me in bed, sank deep into my life, though it was not your goal, the songs you sang still echo in my soul.

And angels watched me because you said a prayer. God's gentle Spirit surrounded me with care. Now as seasons come and go the way that seasons do, what you've sown in time comes back to you.

Each time you blessed me with something warm you made or books you read me and all the times we played, I've held them with both hands when hurtful words were thrown and drawn upon the love that you had sown.

You gave me courage, you cheered at every game. And when I fumbled, you cheered me just the same. As life confused my heart and trouble seemed to grow, I know that you prayed harder, I just know.

And angels watched me because you said a prayer. God's gentle Spirit surrounded me with care. Now as seasons come and go the way that seasons do, what you've sown in time comes back to you.

I'm here to tell you your prayers for me came true and now it's my turn to care and pray for you… That angels watch you, because I say this prayer, God's gentle Spirit surround you with His care. For as seasons come and go the way that seasons do, the love you've sown is coming back to you in time… Just in time.

Like when one sense dulls, the others heighten, as time went on, I became more aware of my mom's spirit than ever before. I knew she was in there. Communication had become limited to tone of voice, eyes and hand gestures, as she had lost her command of words. It was both frightening and frustrating for her. But her spirit was calm and clear, and for a while, every so often, she would surface through the chaos and let me see her essence. It had been well over a year since I had last seen her do that though. Then just weeks after my dad had passed, while I held her hand as she sat in her chair, she turned and focused her eyes on mine, clear as day and with a strong confident voice that I hadn't heard for so, SO long, she looked at me and said, "Don't worry, I'm gonna be okay. God is taking good care of me." She smiled, patted my hand and slipped back into the cocoon of Alzheimer's.

And when all the dust settled, years of care giving, tears and sleepless nights later, I sat up scratching my head, "What just happened?" I cried to God for a new perspective, a new way of seeing my life. I wanted the clarity back that I felt watching my dad step into Glory — to see the truth again of what the realms of living really are. I wanted to know, like the apostle Paul, that to live is Christ, to die is gain and that if I laid down my life here, it would be even more effective there.

Is the war, the battle, only here or are prayer warriors who have stepped into eternity still fighting for God's Kingdom from Heaven's side of things? Are all these folks I'm missing still doing battle for the Kingdom, or are they only cheering the rest of us on like a great cloud of witnesses?

Despite every loss we ever experience here and now, Christ's sacrifice on the cross has gained for us the most unique connection of all time. What looked like the ultimate loss, like God had abandoned His Son and left us all for dead, was actually ultimate Love! By God's grace, through that one grave moment of loss, we have forever gained an eternal life-line to God's heart — a cord that can never be severed, a connection that will never be lost.

So, what feels like loss could really be love. It could be sparing us from heartache worse than the present loss feels. It could be setting us up for a new scene, a brand-new adventure or it might just be giving the storyline enough of a twist to make it really interesting.

Sometimes just the threat of loss is enough to show us where our priorities lie and reveal whether or not we're still trusting God. But then the tree doesn't get cut down and it feels like a resurrection and with it comes new perspectives:

> But whatever was to my profit, I now consider loss for the sake of Christ. What is more, I consider everything loss compared to the surpassing greatness of knowing Christ Jesus, My Lord, for whose sake I have lost all things. I consider them rubbish that I may gain Christ (Philippians 3:7-8).

Exactly one year after my dad left this realm and, as he would say, went home to be with the Lord, I wrote:

> Last night marked a year of Sundays 6:55 PM. I'm overwhelmed by how absurd time really is to a spiritual being. My heart leapt last night at the thought of the soon return of Jesus to reign from Jerusalem and the reunion of loved ones all being raised imperishable, inseparable, completely and fully redeemed! And time will no longer be a factor because it will be unending — measurable only by the rotation of the earth, but not by any changes in our bodies, or loss of loved ones. And for a moment I had a glimpse of eternity again and a new perspective on life. I saw death for what it really is and for what God has rescued us from.

What appears to be the ultimate loss, a final goodbye, is really more like an intermission between acts. It's kinda like our loved ones are now behind the scenes, getting ready for the incredible finale about to happen when the entire cast from all ages past and present, appears for the last scene to take their final curtain call to the applause of multitudes of angels. And the Director Himself gives us a standing ovation, and we bow... lower than we've ever bowed. We bow before

Him. And He says, "Well done, good and faithful servants!" Then we stand to our feet and begin to applaud, and applaud, and applaud Him… and then cheer, and laugh, and cry all together, soon to begin the never-ending sequel, more adventurous than we've even imagined. And of course, it will be the ultimate Happily Ever After (I think He wrote it that way just for me)!

God promises:

> *"I will never say goodbye. I'll forever be your Friend.*
> *If the stars fade in the sky, still My Love for you won't end.*
> *I'm there in your night to comfort you with Light,*
> *until you see the break of day."*

God allows the pain, like a pelting rain,
to wake us back to Life again .

CONCLUSION: Time to Fly

We were created to fly. I'm convinced of it. Think of how many flying dreams you had as a kid. What superhero most fascinated you? I bet they could fly. And didn't you just imagine them swooping down to take you for a ride, just for fun?

We know angels fly or at least they're described as having wings. And if Jesus in His glorious resurrected body could walk through upper-room walls and ascend into the clouds as His disciples watched from the hillside (sounds like flying to me), and Scripture says we will meet Him in the air when He returns, I think we will one day be able to fly again. In the meantime, galloping on the back of a horse is as close to flying without an airplane as I've experienced.

To get back on the horse implies that you failed at something, you fell, or were thrown off at some point, and it hurt. So what's the big deal about getting back on?

I have literally fallen off a horse twice in my life. Both times were on trail rides and a good distance away from the barn. The first time was as a kid on vacation, and the strap that was holding the old army saddle onto the horse actually snapped and I was trotted in slow motion (except for the hitting the ground part) right off the back of the horse, saddle and all. I was young. I bounced. But I had no saddle to get back up onto, so I walked back to the barn, went back to our campsite with my family, waited a couple days, and came back to finish my ride.

The second time was as a 40-something year old on vacation, who hadn't been on a horse in decades. Because I was an experienced rider, or at least I had experienced riding, they gave me a very "spirited" horse that decided to end my ride with a "Hi-Ho-Silver! Away!" reared and then bolted... but without me. The ground definitely gets harder and much farther away the older we get. You know the birds and stars that twirl around a cartoon character's head when it emerges from the imprint in the ground it just made after plummeting through the air? They really do exist. They even tweet. I did not climb back onto the horse that day because I could barely move, never mind climb. It took weeks to recover and it wasn't until a couple years later that I got back on, on a different horse, but I got back on. Was I apprehensive? I gripped the horn of the Western style saddle, which was not my usual practice, and held on for dear life most of the way. But when I was done with the ride, I dismounted (on purpose this time), thanked the horse, and gave him a hug. Then, I thanked God for healing the part of me that only getting back on the horse could heal.

Isaiah 40:31 has been a verse throughout my life that has sustained and encouraged me through some of the roughest points and most challenging moments. The way I first heard it and memorized it was in the King James Version: "But they that wait upon the Lord shall renew their strength. They will mount up with wings as eagles. They shall run and not be weary. They shall walk and not faint."

To get up onto a horse's back is to "mount up." It warms my heart to rethink this verse as mounting a horse and soaring like an eagle, running and not growing weary because I'm being carried by the power beneath me, walking and not being overwhelmed by my surroundings because I can see them from a much higher perspective. Leaning forward, gratefully patting my horse's neck and whispering, "I couldn't do this without you! Thank you!"

When you fall off a horse or life throws you off, recovery can take a few seconds. Recovery can take a life time. There is value in trying again, in getting back on and not giving up. When you've hit the ground hard, "No thanks, God, I think I'd rather walk," is an understandable response. Just know, when you're ready to try again, there will be healing in it waiting for you.

Sharing these pages with you has been like getting back on the horse for me. I didn't think I was ready either. But writing down these words and reading them back were "spirit and life to me." Hearing God dictate them "penetrated my heart" and gathering them all together, finding the glue and making it readable, helped to "set this captive free." Ta-da!

I pray that you, too, have been blessed — that God touched your heart and watered some seedlings. It will all have definitely been worth it, if somehow this book has inspired you to...

get back on the horse again... and fly!

CONCLUSION: Time to Fly

ABOUT THE AUTHOR

For the past 30 years, Sue and her husband, Steve, have served in church leadership and ministry. As lifelong New Englanders, their hearts have always been to see God's Kingdom break ground in the very unique and often hardened soil of New England.

Though Sue has been creatively writing most of her life and has been encouraged by many to publish her work, *Get Back on the Horse?* is in response to God's recent and undeniable prompting, and Sue's growing passion to see people set free from fear, and healed emotionally of past hurts.

ACKNOWLEDGMENTS

As much effort as it takes for the author to pour words onto the page, it takes friends, family and others to give their advice and use their expertise to gently clean up any unwanted spills and splatters made by the author pouring too hastily.

Thank you to those dear friends who helped produce this book through prayers and encouragement. Your words of affirmation counteracted the self-doubt and weariness that happened along the way... more than once.

Christen Scott and Tara Mantho, thank you for taking the time to read this manuscript cover to cover before it was edited down to size. You caught things that had become invisible to me.

Christine McGrory, English teacher and honest friend that you are, your suggestions and corrections were beyond helpful, and so appreciated.

Shawn Downes, your expertise brought professionalism to the finished work. Thanks for being willing to take it on amid your full schedule.

Thank you, Pastor Doug, for many of the ideas and topics of the sketches used in this book (the recorded message segment in "Automated Religion" was all you).

Special thanks to my "sistah," Cindy, for listening to me read through the scribbled rough draft for hours, and for laughing at all the right spots.

Thank you, Kimberlyn, for helping to keep me grounded when technology (and sometimes life) sends me into orbit.

Thanks, Timmy, for so many "hypothetical" examples of life lessons that we learned together... hypothetically of course.

And to my husband, Stevan ~

Thank you for supporting me through a lifetime of projects and "great ideas." Especially when the saddle looks too high off the ground to reach, your love, understanding, and encouragement make it attainable. Thank you for investing in me in so many ways.

This truly is "OUR book."

Sonnet Stanley